Benjamin M.

THE COLLAPSE OF OUR

MONETARY SYSTEM

WITH THE RISE OF AI

Disclaimer

The content of this book represents the personal views, ideas, perceptions, interpretations, and understanding of the author. It is intended solely for informational, educational, and reference purposes. The material presented herein is not offered as professional advice of any kind, including but not limited to legal, financial, psychological, medical, or technical advice.

The views and opinions expressed are entirely those of the author and do not necessarily reflect the positions, beliefs, or policies of any organisation, institution, employer, government body, or individual with which the author may be or may have been affiliated. Any names, events, or scenarios mentioned are referenced in a generalised context for illustrative purposes.

Readers are strongly encouraged to engage with the material critically and independently. While the content draws from the author's personal experiences, interpretations, and observations of the world, it is not intended to be authoritative or definitive. Interpretations may vary, and readers are urged to verify facts, consult relevant sources where appropriate, and draw their own conclusions.

This book also seeks to provoke thought, challenge assumptions, and raise questions about systems, beliefs, and perspectives that shape modern life. It is not written to enforce agreement but to stimulate reflection and encourage deeper inquiry. The author makes no guarantees regarding the accuracy, completeness, or applicability of the content in all contexts and disclaims any liability for actions taken based on the material presented.

Use of the information in this book is at the reader's own discretion and responsibility.

Introduction

I am sure everyone is familiar with the term money. Most of us are using it, chasing it, or making it. It is the next most important thing after oxygen and water, as we need it for every purchase we make. Life would be incredibly harsh without money. So, what exactly is money, despite it being part of our daily lives?

By proper definition, money is an instrument that people use to buy and sell goods and services. Money, as we know it today, even in its digital form, did not always appear to be just numbers in our bank accounts. In the early days, before money even existed in human society, our ancestors traded goods with each other through the method known as bartering, where people had to trade items directly. Take, for example, you have a farm that produces oranges. You cannot be eating oranges every day, as you will have other dietary needs. Your neighbour has a ranch with cows and sheep that produce meat. Through the bartering system, you could technically exchange an orange for a piece of meat, that is, if both sides agree to it. However, your neighbour thinks that his meat is much more valuable due to the effort needed to produce it and the scarcity of the goods, as compared to your oranges, which you could produce by the hundreds easily. He wanted to trade one piece of meat for five oranges. Another person came with some herbs and spices, while a third person came with some salt. Both wanted to exchange their goods for some oranges and meat, but no one could decide the amount needed to exchange the goods between them.

Hence, our ancestors created the idea of using money to measure the value for every good as the standard exchange rate. For example, one orange is worth two shells. One bag of salt is worth five shells. And one piece of meat is worth ten shells. Anyone who wishes to purchase the goods must first gather or exchange their goods with shells to be used for exchanging other goods according to the stipulated amount. Soon, money evolved from simple shells to precious metals that are harder to come by in order to protect its value. The previous metals like gold and silver can be used as exchangeable goods, as they can be melted down to be used for other purposes like jewellery and others.

Paper notes came into existence during the Tang Dynasty in China around the 7th century as promissory notes known commonly as 'flying money'. It was developed to reduce the inconvenience of traders carrying and transporting money and coins, which back then were mostly made from metal. During the Song Dynasty in the 11th century, the Song government institutionalised this practice by issuing state-backed paper currency called *jiaozi*, marking the first known government-issued paper money in history. By the 13th century, under the Yuan Dynasty, paper currency had become widespread. In Europe, paper money appeared in 1661 when Stockholms Banco in Sweden issued the continent's first banknotes, a response to the inefficiencies of bulky metal coins. Britain followed with the establishment of the Bank of England in 1694, which issued notes backed by gold deposits, laying the foundation for modern central banking.

When individuals, groups, or companies accumulated more money than they required, they began lending to those in need. It is likely that this practice started innocently, much like parents providing their children with funds as down payments on cars or houses, with the expectation of repayment once the children began earning. Over time, however, someone motivated by greed introduced the idea of charging interest, turning lending into a 'service of convenience'. Given the shared nature of human societies, the practice of lending and borrowing money, along with charging interest commonly called usury, has existed for thousands of years across many civilisations and eras.

In ancient Mesopotamia, as early as 3000 BCE, loans typically took the form of grain or silver, with interest rates regulated by legal codes such as the Code of Hammurabi. This early regulation indicates an awareness of the potential societal impacts of lending practices. Similarly, in ancient Greece, philosopher Aristotle condemned usury, arguing that money should serve as a medium of exchange rather than a tool for generating profit through interest. Roman law permitted interest-bearing loans, but imposed caps to prevent excessive rates, reflecting a balance between economic activity and social equity. During the medieval period, Christian doctrine influenced by biblical teachings prohibited usury, viewing it as morally reprehensible.

Such services formed the basis of modern-day banking, where the business revolves around taking deposits and then lending the money to customers to profit from the interest. As time went by, banks began to print money that they did not have to fund wars and other major events. In North America, the Massachusetts Bay Colony introduced paper currency in 1690 to finance military expeditions. Although over-issuance during the Revolutionary War later caused the collapse of Continental Currency, the system of paper money persisted. By the 20th century, most major economies had transitioned from metal-backed notes to fiat currency. This culminated in the end of the gold standard in 1971, when the United States ceased dollar-to-gold convertibility, solidifying paper money's role as a value system based entirely on government trust.

The abuse of the system by central banks led to the introduction of cryptocurrencies like Bitcoin, Ethereum, and dozens of meme coins. The position of currency or money as we know it as the dominant instrument of trade has begun showing cracks in the system. The recent rise of AI has further changed the definition of money.

So, is this the end of money in our society? Or will it undergo a significant transformation, similar to how AI is going to forever change human society? How will the concept of value evolve in a world where digital assets and artificial intelligence dominate? Will traditional currencies maintain their relevance, or will they become relics of a bygone era? Could decentralised finance and cryptocurrencies reshape economic power structures, placing control back into the hands of individuals? What risks and opportunities will emerge as money becomes increasingly abstract and intangible? How might these changes affect wealth distribution, social equity, and access to resources? Finally, what role will governments and regulatory bodies play in managing or resisting these sweeping changes to the nature of money itself?

A Bit of History

The Foundations of International Banking: The Knights Templar and Their Financial Legacy

Let us revisit a bit about the origins of international banking to better understand how the practice started. I used to have the impression that the first international bank, or at least the concept and practice, was started by a group of merchants or traders who made so much money that they began treating money as tradable commodities. This idea stuck with me for a while until the internet came into existence and information was just a click away. My view changed when I learnt that the first verifiable concept was developed by the Knights Templar while reading about the information and stories of the Crusades.

Although they are often romanticised as warrior-monks, the Knights Templar were far more than just a military religious order. They were skilled administrators, resourceful financiers, and early innovators of complex systems that laid the very groundwork for what we now understand as modern international banking. Yes, this might come as a surprise, but these were not the battle-hungry, reckless knights driven solely by bloodlust and a thirst for combat, as they are frequently portrayed in popular films and literature. Instead, the Templars constituted a multifaceted monastic order with deep commitments, fulfilling a variety of crucial roles throughout the Crusades, particularly in establishing some of the earliest known banking practices.

Their financial operations arose out of practical necessity. Christian pilgrims, venturing on long, arduous journeys to Jerusalem, faced numerous dangers and uncertainties. They required not only physical protection from the perils along the route but also a secure method to safeguard their funds while travelling through hostile territories and foreign lands. In response to this urgent need, the Templars developed innovative financial instruments and systems that allowed pilgrims to deposit funds at one location and withdraw equivalent amounts elsewhere, thereby reducing the risk of theft or loss during their travels. This early form of banking provided a foundation for trust and efficiency, enabling trade and movement on a scale previously unimaginable. The Templars' banking practices were groundbreaking in their time, combining religious dedication with pragmatic financial acumen, and their influence extended well beyond their military exploits, ultimately shaping the economic landscape of medieval Europe and beyond.

By the twelfth and thirteenth centuries, the Knights Templar had established an extensive network of commandries, estates, and fortresses stretching across Europe and the Middle East, from England and France all the way to the Levant. This vast network offered not only crucial military security but also a remarkably sophisticated infrastructure for managing money, property, and other valuable assets. According to Barber (1994), as many as 90 per cent of the Templars were non-combatants. These members specialised in logistics, accounting, administration, and financial management, while only a small fraction were highly trained knights who actively engaged in combat during the Crusades.

The increasing need to move large sums of money into the Levant to support military campaigns, as well as to facilitate the acquisition of land, property, and other assets by wealthy Europeans in the region, drove the Templars to develop what is arguably the first truly international financial system. This early system offered services that remain foundational to modern banking practices. Among these services were:

- **Letters of credit:** A pilgrim could deposit funds at a Templar preceptory in Europe, receive a coded document and withdraw an equivalent value in the Holy Land. This dramatically reduced the risk of carrying coinage on dangerous routes and saved the time and effort of moving heavy coins over long distances, as coins were made mainly from metal.

- **Estate management:** The Templars administered vast estates and revenues on behalf of nobles, monarchs, and the Church, often acting as custodians of wealth. In other words, they were medieval property management agents or early real estate investment trusts (REITs).

- **Monetary transfers:** Funds could be transferred between kingdoms using the Templars' infrastructure, avoiding the risks and inefficiencies of physical transport.

- **Safe deposits:** Kings, nobles, and even popes entrusted their valuables to the Templars for safekeeping.

Their network resembled a proto-banking institution. According to Nicholson (2001), by the mid-thirteenth century the Templars had become key financial agents for European monarchs, including King Louis the Ninth of France and King Henry the Third of England. Their prominence in finance grew to such an extent that the French Crown, deeply indebted to them, eventually took action against the order in 1307 under the pretence of heresy, leading to its dissolution.

Their financial practices were carefully recorded, standardised, and internally audited, reflecting an early form of bureaucratic professionalism that was rare during that period. While not a bank in the modern sense, the order's organisational structure and operations possessed features that would later be formalised in contemporary banking systems.

The effectiveness and efficiency of the system were influenced and adopted by another banking giant later in the fifteenth century.

The Medici Bank, founded in 1397 by Giovanni di Bicci de' Medici, emerged in a Europe already familiar with the financial innovations of the Templars. However, the Medici family introduced their own innovations, including branch banking, double-entry bookkeeping, and trade finance. These innovations built upon the Templars' earlier model, refining a system that generated enormous profits from interest.

Although the Medici family had prior experience in trade and smaller-scale money-lending, Giovanni shifted the family's focus primarily to banking. He capitalised on his existing connections and leveraged Florence's prominence as a leading trade hub. During its early years, the bank concentrated on managing commercial transactions for Florentine merchants, particularly in the lucrative wool trade, while also providing financial management services to local elites. Giovanni cultivated a reputation for prudence and reliability, distinguishing himself from earlier, more reckless banking families such as the Bardi and Peruzzi. Their spectacular failures in the mid-fourteenth century served as a cautionary tale for future bankers. One of Giovanni's earliest strategic moves was to build strong ties with the Papacy, thereby securing a key role in managing Church finances.

Under Giovanni's leadership and subsequently that of his son, Cosimo de' Medici, the bank expanded significantly beyond Florence. Rather than depending solely on agents, they created a network of semi-autonomous branches in prominent European financial and political centres. These included Rome, frequently the most profitable due to its papal connections, as well as Venice, Milan, Geneva, Lyon, Avignon, Bruges, and London.

Each branch operated as a limited-term partnership. The Florence headquarters, known as the *tavola*, held the majority stake, typically fifty per cent or more. The local branch manager, referred to as the governatore, was a trusted junior partner who held a smaller share and contributed his own capital. This structure motivated branch managers to manage their operations profitably, while ultimate control and most profits remained with Florence.

This decentralised yet controlled framework allowed the bank to engage effectively with local markets and manage risks across a vast geographical area. The Medici ensured regular correspondence and rigorous accounting practices to maintain oversight and communication throughout the network.

The Medici Bank offered a range of sophisticated services that were advanced for its time:

- **Deposit Banking:** The bank accepted funds for safekeeping from merchants, nobles, and high-ranking church officials. This service provided security for wealth that otherwise faced risks from theft or political instability.

- **Loans**: Credit was extended to merchants to finance trade ventures and, importantly, large sums were lent to monarchs, popes, and political figures. This lending was a key source of influence for the Medici family, who carefully diversified their portfolio to avoid the pitfalls of earlier banks, which failed largely due to excessive exposure to sovereign debt.

- **Trade Finance (Bills of Exchange):** Central to the bank's operations, bills of exchange allowed the Medici to facilitate international payments without the physical shipment of bullion. By manipulating the embedded exchange rates, the bank earned profits through interest while skilfully navigating around contemporary usury laws. This financial innovation was vital for the wool, silk, and spice trades that dominated international commerce.

- **Papal Banking:** The Rome branch of the Medici Bank managed the Pope's financial affairs. This included transferring substantial revenues from across Christendom, such as taxes, tithes, and indulgence payments. The bank also oversaw papal investments and administered the exclusive monopoly on Tolfa alum, a critical material in textile dyeing. The privileges granted by the Pope allowed the Medici to command significant profits and influence within the textile industry.

- **Currency Exchange:** Operating within a Europe crowded with numerous coinages, the bank profited by managing the complex exchange rates, turning currency conversion into a lucrative business line.

- **Investment Management:** Acting in a capacity resembling modern private banking, the Medici managed assets and commercial ventures for their wealthy clientele, expanding their influence beyond traditional banking.

- **Double-Entry Bookkeeping:** Although not the originators of this method, the Medici systematically applied double-entry bookkeeping throughout their branch network. This practice enabled meticulous tracking of profits, losses, assets, and liabilities both locally and centrally, proving indispensable in managing the complexities of such a widespread financial enterprise.

The Medici Bank reached unprecedented levels of success, propelling the Medici family into the political and economic elite of Europe. While Giovanni had laid the foundation, it was Cosimo who truly expanded the Medici influence, not just in terms of wealth but also of power. Cosimo leveraged the Bank's vast resources to shape political alliances, solidify his control over Florence, and provide substantial loans to both rulers and the Papacy.

Rather than simply relying on revenues from trade or local business, Cosimo used his financial reach to extend the family's political influence far beyond Florence. He made loans to kings, popes, and other prominent political figures from the Bank, using these financial ties as leverage in his political dealings. His control of the Bank gave him the ability to influence decisions at the highest levels, making him one of the most powerful figures in Europe despite holding no formal political office.

Cosimo's financial genius lay not only in the management of the Bank but also in his strategic use of Medici wealth to patronise the arts, which would later become one of the family's most enduring legacies. His commissions helped fuel the flourishing of Renaissance art and culture and his financial support enabled the production of some of the era's greatest works.

Under Cosimo's patronage, the Medici family commissioned Filippo Brunelleschi to design and complete the great dome of Santa Maria del Fiore, oversaw Sandro Botticelli's creation of The Birth of Venus with its ethereal beauty embodying both civic pride and personal devotion, and celebrated Michelangelo's unveiling of David, declaring it Florence's guardian. Each masterpiece not only demonstrated unparalleled artistic innovation but also served as a form of soft power, reinforcing Medici influence and shaping Florence's identity as the cradle of the Renaissance.

Through this combination of wealth, strategic financial alliances and cultural patronage, the Medici family established their dominance in Florence and beyond. They were not just bankers; they were power brokers, political masterminds and cultural patrons, whose influence shaped the course of European history.

However, the Medici Bank's success was not destined to last forever. Under Lorenzo de' Medici, known as Lorenzo the Magnificent, the Bank began to experience a significant decline. While Lorenzo's political influence and patronage of the arts flourished, the Bank suffered from a combination of internal and external pressures. Mismanagement by branch managers, who operated with increasing autonomy and often with little oversight from the central leadership in Florence, was one of the first cracks in the Bank's once-solid foundation.

Charles the Bold, Duke of Burgundy, provides a telling case of the Bank's overreach. The substantial credit extended to him ignored the era's political volatility. When he failed to repay, his duchy's collapse wiped out much of the Bank's capital. Beyond Burgundy, the Bank had also overextended itself by funding costly wars and estates across Italy. These decisions deepened the Bank's losses and undermined its stability.

As the Medici family became more embroiled in the political and cultural affairs of Florence, their attention shifted away from the day-to-day operations of the Bank. With Lorenzo focused on consolidating political power and patronising the arts, the Bank's financial stability took a back seat. The combination of shifting political tides in Florence, marked by the overthrow of the Medici family in 1494, and across Europe, coupled with internal mismanagement, proved disastrous.

The political upheaval in Florence, along with the rise of new rival banking institutions, contributed to the Bank's eventual collapse. In 1494, the Medici Bank ceased to operate, its once vast influence diminished by the very forces that had previously helped it thrive.

The Medici Bank left a profound imprint on the evolution of modern banking by pioneering the systematisation of branch banking. It established a strong network that spanned Europe, with each branch operating semi-independently while still under the control of the

Florence headquarters. This model of decentralisation, together with the extensive use of double-entry bookkeeping, was invaluable for maintaining financial oversight across its international operations. Its sophisticated management of bills of exchange and international credit cemented its power and influence, demonstrating how a private financial institution could expand its reach across Europe, facilitate complex transactions and even exercise political power through its financial dealings.

While the Medici Bank's downfall came long before the Rothschild banking dynasty emerged, there are striking similarities between the two. The Rothschilds, who rose to prominence in the eighteenth and nineteenth centuries, operated in a vastly different era. The world in which they thrived was shaped by the Industrial Revolution and the rise of modern nation-states. Despite the temporal and contextual differences, the two banking families shared certain traits that linked their legacies.

Both the Medici and the Rothschild families built powerful, family-controlled banking networks that reached across the most important cities in Europe. The Medici used their vast connections to influence political decisions and amass immense wealth, while the Rothschilds found similar success centuries later by providing loans to national governments and playing a crucial role in state finance. These similarities were not coincidental. Both families understood that financial power could serve as a tool not only for making profit, but also for shaping the political direction of Europe. By controlling large-scale capital and maintaining trusted partnerships across borders, they turned their private banks into instruments of political influence and long-lasting historical impact.

One of the key advantages shared by both the Medici and the Rothschild families was their privileged access to vital information. The Medici, operating across a vast banking network that spanned multiple cities, were able to gather intelligence unavailable to most. Their access to commercial, political, and diplomatic correspondence gave them a strategic edge in both financial and political decision-making. Centuries later, the Rothschilds achieved similar dominance by capitalising on the rapid communication afforded by the telegraph. While the scale and speed of their operations were vastly different, the principle remained the same. The Medici relied on traditional couriers, whereas the Rothschilds employed telegraphic systems. Yet both families mastered the use of information as a decisive instrument for financial power and influence.

The Medici were the pioneers of Renaissance finance, creating an integrated system that enabled them to manage international banking on a scale never seen before. Their network of semi-independent branches, strict accounting oversight, and use of double-entry bookkeeping allowed them to maintain control over complex financial operations spread across Europe. This structure provided the basis for more sophisticated banking institutions that would later emerge with the growth of industrial capitalism and global commerce. The Rothschilds, centuries later, inherited the principles the Medici had established and adapted them to meet the demands of a rapidly changing world. Their operations expanded across a modern economic landscape shaped by industrialisation, national competition, and evolving financial markets.

While the context of their activities differed profoundly, the underlying strategies of influence, information control, and international reach bore remarkable similarities. The Medici laid the foundational blueprint, and the Rothschilds expanded it into a financial system capable of navigating the complexities of the modern global age.

The Rise of International Banks

The successes of both the Knight Templars and the Medici Banks in transforming the financial landscape paved the way for the international banks led by the prominent Rothschild family, who established their influence and power by funding wars and governments worldwide.

Following in the footsteps of the Medici family, Mayer Amschel Rothschild and his five sons expanded on medieval banking innovations to establish a truly international bank. They opened offices in Frankfurt, London, Paris, Vienna and Naples, connecting them through a trusted network of agents and swift couriers. By financing the coalitions opposing Napoleon, underwriting government loans across Europe and advising monarchs on fiscal policy, they not only replicated the success of the Medici family but surpassed it in many respects. Their unparalleled power, wealth and political influence grew steadily. Their expertise in placing sovereign bonds at favourable rates enabled states to finance wars and rebuild during peacetime, while granting the Rothschilds privileged access to insider information. As they expanded into funding railways, canals and emerging industries, they helped shape the infrastructure of the modern world. Through these efforts, the Rothschilds transformed banking from a regional craft into a global enterprise.

The early seventeenth century saw the emergence of investment banks, institutions that provided financing for large-scale commercial projects. This period also witnessed the establishment of the Bank of England in 1694, which marked a significant development in the evolution of modern banking systems. The Bank of England was created primarily to manage the national debt incurred from the wars of the time, but its formation also introduced a centralised institution capable of overseeing and regulating monetary policy in Britain. It became a model for central banks later established in other countries.

Expansion of International Banking in the 19th Century

As global trade surged throughout the nineteenth century, particularly with the momentum of the Industrial Revolution, the need for international banking intensified. The expansion of British imperialism, alongside growing trade networks stretching across Asia, Africa, and the Americas, spurred the establishment of new international financial institutions. Amidst this transformation, the Rothschild family emerged as a dominant force in global finance, extending credit not only to governments but also to burgeoning businesses across Europe. Their vast banking empire became instrumental in underwriting major infrastructure ventures, from sprawling railway lines carving through continents to pioneering energy systems powering industrial growth worldwide.

The Rothschilds were not the sole influential family in the rise of international banking. In the United States, J. P. Morgan emerged as a titan of finance during the late nineteenth and early twentieth centuries, shaping the contours of both national and global economies. His firm, J. P. Morgan & Co., became a powerhouse in domestic and international banking, providing crucial capital that propelled America's industrial giants in steel, railroads, and electricity. Crossing national boundaries, Morgan's firm took an active role in financing ventures across Europe and Latin America, underwriting vast infrastructure projects and facilitating vital cross-border investments. Through masterful consolidation of rival companies, deft debt restructuring, and subtle financial diplomacy, Morgan's influence reached far beyond the marble halls of Wall Street, shaping the economic landscape of the modern world.

The Establishment of International Financial Institutions

The need for a more coordinated international financial system became evident in the aftermath of the First World War. The conflict had left many European countries heavily indebted, and the existing global financial structure proved inadequate for maintaining long-term stability. In response, efforts were made to reorganise international monetary relations and foster greater cooperation among central banks. One significant outcome was the creation of the Bank for International Settlements (BIS) in 1930. The BIS was established to promote monetary and financial stability, facilitate dialogue and collaboration among central banks, and serve as a bank for central banks by offering services and support across national boundaries.

Following the devastation of the Second World War, a new global economic order emerged under the Bretton Woods System. At the Bretton Woods Conference in 1944, major economic powers agreed to establish the International Monetary Fund (IMF) and the World Bank. These institutions were designed to ensure global financial stability and support the reconstruction of war-torn economies. The IMF aimed to regulate exchange rates, provide short-term financial assistance, and promote balance of payments stability, while the World Bank focused on long-term development through investment in infrastructure and poverty reduction. Together, they laid the groundwork for a more structured and rules-based international financial system. The establishment of the IMF and the World Bank marked a turning point in the evolution of global economic governance, as both institutions continue to play a central role in the regulation of international finance.

Transition into Modern International Banks

The latter half of the twentieth century and the beginning of the twenty-first century witnessed the rise of multinational financial corporations and investment banks operating across national borders. Institutions such as Citigroup, HSBC, and Goldman Sachs expanded their operations globally, playing a key role in the increasing integration of financial markets and national economies. Through mergers, acquisitions, and strategic partnerships, these firms established a presence in major financial centres around the world and became central to the functioning of the global financial system. The advent of new technologies, including digital banking platforms and online financial services, further extended their reach. These innovations allowed international banks to offer financial products and services to individuals and businesses in virtually every region, transforming the scale and speed at which global finance could operate.

The Central Bank

After World War II, the international economic landscape was restructured by the Bretton Woods Agreement in 1944, signed by forty-four Allied nations in the town of Bretton Woods, New Hampshire. The agreement aimed to create a new framework for global monetary stability, recognising the need for clear rules on international trade and currency exchange following years of economic turmoil.

Under Bretton Woods, the cornerstone of the global monetary system was a fixed exchange rate regime. Each country agreed to peg its currency to the US dollar, which itself was convertible into gold at a rate of thirty-five dollars per ounce. The United States, holding the largest gold reserves, was effectively seen as the anchor of this system. The principle was straightforward: by linking currencies to the dollar, countries could maintain stability in international trade, ensuring that exchange rates remained predictable, which would encourage investment and support long-term economic growth.

For nearly three decades, the system appeared effective. It facilitated the rapid recovery of Europe and Japan, the global spread of trade, and an era of unprecedented growth in the global economy. This period witnessed the rebuilding of nations, a surge in international commerce, and the rise of new economic powers on the world stage. By the mid-1960s, however, the foundations of Bretton Woods began to show significant signs of strain as economic imbalances, coupled with mounting political pressures, began to erode the stability of the system.

One of the major flaws in the system lay in its reliance on the US dollar's convertibility to gold at a fixed rate, which placed immense pressure on the United States' gold reserves. In the early 1960s, the US, having experienced significant post-war economic expansion, faced mounting military expenditures due to its involvement in the Vietnam War. The financial burden grew further due to the costs of maintaining global political influence during the Cold War. At the same time, domestic social spending under the Great Society programmes added to the strain on the nation's finances. As the US government began running large budget deficits, its gold reserves dwindled, leading to growing concerns among foreign governments and investors about the US's ability to maintain the dollar's convertibility.

Foreign countries, particularly in Europe and Asia, grew increasingly wary of holding US dollars, knowing that the amount of gold held by the US could not support the growing supply of dollars in circulation. As a result, many countries began demanding gold in exchange for their dollars, which only exacerbated the US's reserve problems. By the late 1960s, the US was facing a balance of payments deficit, importing more than it was exporting, further inflating the global supply of dollars. As more dollars circulated internationally, the US's gold reserves continued to decline steadily, deepening concerns about the system's sustainability. The situation worsened in 1971 as the US found itself in an untenable position. The growing demand for gold from foreign governments, combined with the rising global supply of US dollars, placed immense pressure on the US's gold reserves. Faced with mounting economic challenges, President Richard Nixon took the unprecedented step on 15 August 1971 of suspending the convertibility of the US dollar to gold, effectively ending the Bretton Woods system. This move, known as the Nixon Shock, marked a pivotal moment in the history of international finance. Nixon's decision was driven by the realisation that the US could no longer maintain the gold standard without depleting its gold reserves and that it had become increasingly difficult to uphold the dollar's value in relation to other currencies.

The suspension of the dollar's convertibility into gold was not initially framed as a permanent abandonment of the gold standard but rather as a temporary measure to address the mounting economic pressures. However, in the aftermath of the Nixon Shock, the Bretton Woods system began to unravel. Without the anchor of gold, the US dollar was allowed to float freely against other currencies. Other nations followed suit and the world transitioned to a floating exchange rate system, where currencies were no longer pegged to gold or any other fixed asset. Instead, they were valued based on market forces of supply and demand. This shift marked the beginning of the modern era of fiat currency, where the value of money is determined by trust and government-backed guarantees rather than a tangible commodity like gold.

With the decoupling of the dollar from gold, central banks worldwide were charged with novel responsibilities and endowed with enhanced monetary policy instruments, including open-market operations to fine-tune short-term interest rates, adjustable reserve requirement ratios to influence bank lending capacity, discount-window facilities to provide emergency liquidity and targeted foreign-exchange interventions to mitigate excessive currency fluctuations. The Federal Reserve and its counterparts thus reoriented their mandates, shifting their primary objectives from upholding fixed exchange parities to pursuing price stability through systematic interest-rate adjustments, maintaining orderly exchange-rate regimes within a managed-float framework and fostering sustainable economic expansion by calibrating monetary growth to real-economy indicators.

Under Arthur Burns, the Federal Reserve initially struggled to manage the transition. The immediate consequences of the collapse of the Bretton Woods system were turbulent compared with the stability of the post-World War II period. Inflation began to rise globally after oil prices more than quadrupled during the 1973 oil crisis, and a period of stagflation, a combination of high inflation and stagnant economic growth, followed. In the United States, unemployment reached 9.0% in May 1975, while inflation climbed to 11.3% by 1979 and peaked at 13.5% in 1980. The US economy consequently faced a difficult decade defined by high unemployment and persistent inflationary pressures.

By the late 1970s, under the leadership of Paul Volcker, the Federal Reserve took drastic measures to combat the rapidly accelerating inflation that was severely affecting the economy. Volcker, appointed as Fed chairman in 1979, was determined to break the back of the inflationary cycle that had plagued the US throughout the decade. His aggressive monetary policies involved sharply increasing interest rates, which climbed to nearly 20%, a level previously unseen in modern times, as part of his effort to curb runaway inflation and stabilise the economy. Although this strategy initially resulted in severe economic pain, with rising unemployment and a slowdown in industrial output, it eventually led to a significant reduction in inflation rates. In the longer term, these measures restored the Federal Reserve's credibility as a powerful institution capable of controlling inflation and ensuring price stability, earning Volcker respect for his unwavering stance, even though his policies were highly controversial at the time.

The Role of Central Banks and Monetary Policy

Central banks are at the core of modern economies, serving as the institutions responsible for managing monetary policy, regulating the money supply, and aiming to ensure economic stability. The principal objective of central banking is typically to maintain price stability, generally understood as low and stable inflation, and to support conditions conducive to sustainable economic growth and high employment. Central banks, such as the Federal Reserve in the United States and the Bank of England in the UK, work towards these goals primarily through the application of key monetary policy instruments, including the setting of official interest rates and the management of commercial banks' reserves.

Here's some of the key functions of a central bank:

1. **Issuing Currency:** Central banks typically possess the exclusive authority to issue banknotes and coins within a country. This function ensures there is sufficient physical currency promoting liquidity for everyday transactions and forms a crucial part of the overall money supply which central banks manage to influence economic conditions.

2. **Monetary Policy**: A primary role of central banks is the formulation and implementation of monetary policy. This involves managing interest rates and credit conditions to achieve macroeconomic objectives such as controlling inflation, maintaining the stability of the national currency and fostering sustainable economic growth and employment. Monetary policy can be adjusted to be expansionary, stimulating economic activity typically during downturns, or contractionary, aiming to curb inflation and prevent an economy from overheating.

3. **Regulation of Inflation:** Central banks often operate with specific inflation targets aiming to keep inflation low, stable and predictable, thereby preventing the damaging economic consequences of hyperinflation or sustained deflation. A common target in many developed economies is around 2 percent annually, although this can differ based on national circumstances. Through their monetary policy tools, particularly adjustments to benchmark interest rates which influence borrowing costs and credit availability throughout the economy, central banks strive to steer inflation towards these targets.

4. **Interest Rate Control:** Central banks significantly influence economic activity by setting key policy interest rates, such as the rate at which commercial banks can borrow from the central bank or the target rate for interbank lending. Changes to these benchmark rates ripple through the financial system, affecting broader borrowing and saving rates for individuals and

businesses. Lowering policy rates generally encourages borrowing for investment and consumption, potentially stimulating growth, while raising rates tends to dampen borrowing and spending which can help to control inflation when the economy is growing too quickly.

Monetary Policy Tools

Monetary policy consists of actions undertaken by a central bank to regulate the money supply and credit conditions with the aim of achieving its macroeconomic objectives. Its primary focus lies in managing inflation and supporting both economic stability and growth. This process involves influencing the cost of money, such as interest rates, and its availability throughout the economy, thereby shaping borrowing, spending, and investment decisions.

Central banks utilise several key tools to implement monetary policy. These instruments enable them to influence the money supply, credit conditions, and overall economic activity with the goal of achieving their macroeconomic objectives, such as price stability and sustainable growth.

- **Policy Interest Rates:** Central banks set or influence key short-term interest rates, including the rate at which they lend to commercial banks and the target rate for overnight interbank lending. Adjusting this benchmark rate alters the cost of borrowing for commercial banks, which then affects the wider range of interest rates offered to consumers and businesses for loans and savings. A reduction in the policy interest rate tends to lower borrowing costs throughout the economy, encouraging spending and investment, thereby stimulating economic activity. Conversely, increasing the policy interest rate generally makes borrowing more expensive. This helps to dampen spending and investment, slows an overheating economy, and curbs inflationary pressures.

- **Open Market Operations (OMOs):** These involve the central bank buying and selling financial assets, most commonly government securities such as bonds, in the open market with commercial banks. When the central bank purchases securities from banks, it credits the banks' reserve accounts, injecting liquidity—central bank money—into the banking system. This increases banks' capacity to lend, potentially lowering interest rates and expanding the money supply. When the central bank sells securities to banks, it withdraws liquidity from the system as banks pay using their reserves. This restricts lending capacity and tends to push interest rates upward. OMOs serve as a primary and frequently used tool for managing the money supply and keeping short-term market interest rates close to the central bank's policy target.

- **Reserve Requirements:** Central banks require commercial banks to hold a minimum percentage of their customer deposits in reserve. This is known as the reserve requirement or reserve ratio. These reserves must usually be held as cash in bank vaults or deposits with the central bank. By changing this required percentage, the central bank can influence the funds banks have available to lend. Raising the reserve requirement reduces funds available for lending, potentially slowing credit growth, while lowering it releases reserves, enabling banks to lend more. Despite its effectiveness, changes to reserve requirements are generally considered a blunt instrument and are used less frequently than policy rate adjustments or OMOs in many major economies today.

For central banks to carry out their roles effectively, maintaining the trust of the public and financial markets is absolutely crucial. This trust underpins the entire monetary system, particularly in modern economies that rely on fiat currency. Unlike commodity-backed money, fiat currency has no intrinsic value. Its worth depends entirely on the confidence placed in the issuing authority, the central bank's ability to manage the economy prudently, and the perceived stability of the national economy itself.

- **Independence:** A significant degree of operational independence from short-term political pressures is widely regarded as essential for central banks to function effectively over the long term. If central banks were subject to direct control or manipulation by elected officials, there would be a risk of monetary policy being skewed toward short-term political aims. This might involve artificially stimulating the economy before elections to create the illusion of prosperity, which could lead to higher inflation or economic instability later on. Political interference of this nature would erode the credibility of the central bank and threaten the long-term stability of the currency and the economy it supports. Thus, many countries establish legal frameworks that guarantee the autonomy of their central banks, allowing them to focus on their core mandates without undue political influence.

- **Transparency and Communication:** Modern central banking increasingly emphasises transparency and clear communication with both the public and financial markets. Central banks now actively disclose their assessments of economic conditions and policy intentions to shape market expectations and reduce uncertainty. One key strategy is the use of 'forward guidance', where the central bank provides explicit indications about its likely future policy moves based on current economic outlooks. This guidance helps businesses, investors, and households plan their borrowing, spending, and investment decisions with greater confidence, making monetary policy more effective. Additionally, central banks promote openness by publishing minutes from policy meetings, issuing regular reports, and holding press conferences. Such practices enhance accountability and foster public trust by providing insight into the decision-making process and clarifying the bank's objectives.

While independence and transparency are presented as ideals for effective central banking, they also raise complex questions. How independent can or should a central bank truly be in a democracy, and to whom is it ultimately accountable when its decisions profoundly affect citizens' lives? Does increased transparency always lead to better outcomes, or could it sometimes constrain the central bank's ability to act decisively or manage market sensitivities effectively? Furthermore, given the inherent uncertainties in economic forecasting, how much confidence should be placed in forward guidance, and what happens when communicated intentions must inevitably change? Finally, considering recent global economic challenges, how effectively can central banks truly manage inflation and stability using the tools available to them, especially when facing shocks originating outside the traditional monetary sphere?

How does The Economy Work?

Having outlined the foundational concepts of money and the central institutions governing its management, we will now analyse the broader economy to understand how money functions within this system. To deepen this exploration, we will assess specific mechanisms such as monetary flows, market interactions, and the interplay between fiscal policy and economic stability. This will include evaluating how variables like inflation, interest rates, and employment levels are influenced by, and in turn shape, monetary dynamics.

How the Basic Economy Works

The economy is a system that organises how a society produces, distributes, and consumes resources. It involves individuals, groups, perhaps forming early businesses, and potentially some form of collective organisation interacting to meet needs through the creation and exchange of goods, services, and eventually money. At its foundation, this system relies on the core principles of production, trade, and the interplay of supply and demand to function. Production occurs when individuals apply labour, utilise natural resources, and employ capital, which includes tools, simple machinery, or even improved land, to create goods such as food or clothing, or to provide services such as basic healthcare or transportation. These goods and services are then made available through various forms of exchange to consumers who need or desire them. Consumer demand, often expressed through purchasing if money is used, signals to producers which items are valued and potentially warrant increased production. Trade facilitates this essential exchange process, initially perhaps through direct bartering but more efficiently through the use of money once it develops. Money simplifies transactions immensely by acting as a widely accepted medium of exchange, a common unit of account for measuring value and a durable store of wealth. Within this framework, prices typically emerge where the available supply of a good or service meets the level of demand for it. If an item is scarce yet highly desired, its price tends to rise, which in turn provides an incentive for producers to increase its supply if they have the capability to do so.

For example, a farmer may cultivate crops and sell them at a local market, using the income generated to purchase necessary tools or other essential goods. Similarly, a carpenter might utilise raw timber to manufacture furniture, which could be traded directly for foodstuffs or sold in exchange for money. These transactions facilitate the circulation of goods, services, and resources within the community, ensuring that economic activity remains continuous and interconnected.

As previously discussed in the previous chapter, money substantially reduces the limitations of barter systems. Barter requires a coincidence of wants, meaning one must find another party who both possesses the desired goods and desires the goods one offers. Money, on the other hand, acts as a universally accepted medium of exchange, greatly improving the efficiency and scale of trade.

Historically, such economies relied on tangible forms of wealth, including precious metals, fertile land, and livestock. Economic expansion depended largely on saving and investment. Individuals or households would set aside a portion of their earnings or surplus production and use these savings to increase future productive capacity. This might involve financing the construction of infrastructure such as watermills or acquiring improved tools and equipment. Through these investments, productivity could be enhanced, increasing the community's overall wealth.

Although economic activity was primarily private, early governments or community organisations often intervened. They might regulate trade, construct infrastructure such as roads and bridges, or levy taxes to fund collective needs. These interventions helped maintain the economic framework and supported growth by providing necessary public goods and oversight.

This system, often called the "real economy", links wealth creation and value directly to physical output, tangible assets, and productive services. Compared to more complex financial systems, it generally fosters slower but more stable economic development. Growth depends on concrete investments and outputs, which tend to produce predictable and enduring results over time.

The Current Debt-Centric Economy

Contemporary economies across the globe operate largely on a debt-centric model where borrowing and the availability of credit are the primary drivers of economic activity. Unlike the basic economic model rooted predominantly in existing tangible wealth, this system relies heavily on leverage through debt, essentially promises to pay in the future, to stimulate current spending and foster growth. Commercial banks play a pivotal role, as they create a significant portion of the money supply through the process of lending. For instance, when an individual borrows $20,000 for a car, the bank typically does not distribute cash directly from its vaults or existing deposits. Instead, it credits the borrower's account with the loan amount through accounting entries, thereby expanding the overall money supply. This mechanism of credit creation enables households to purchase homes using mortgages, allows businesses to finance expansion through loans or by issuing bonds, and permits governments to fund public spending and infrastructure projects by issuing sovereign debt. The continuous need to service this vast web of debt, meaning paying interest and repaying principal, necessitates ongoing economic activity and income generation. Furthermore, the system often relies on the creation of new loans exceeding repayments to maintain overall economic expansion and prevent deflationary pressures. Central banks, such as the Federal

Reserve or the Bank of England, attempt to manage this dynamic environment primarily by adjusting key interest rates. Lower rates are intended to encourage borrowing and economic activity, whilst higher rates are designed to curb borrowing and control inflation. Consequently, much economic focus and value generation within this system centres on financial instruments like stocks, bonds, mortgages, and complex derivatives, often alongside or sometimes seemingly detached from the production of physical goods and services.

A family might borrow $400,000 via a mortgage to purchase a house. This single transaction stimulates activity in construction, real estate services, and related industries, while the family commits to repayments typically stretching over decades. Similarly, a national government could issue billions in bonds, effectively borrowing on a vast scale, to finance the construction of new schools or hospitals, with repayment obligations met through future tax revenues or often by refinancing through issuing further debt. This reliance on credit has propelled total global debt, encompassing household, corporate, and government borrowing, to levels vastly exceeding annual global economic output, often estimated to exceed $300 trillion. While this model can significantly accelerate economic growth and development by bringing forward future spending, it simultaneously introduces substantial risks. If borrowers default on their obligations on a large scale, as witnessed during the global financial crisis triggered by the US housing market crash around 2008, the value of assets used as collateral can collapse, potentially triggering widespread financial instability and severe economic downturns. Furthermore, such a system can contribute to wealth concentration, as returns from lending tend to accumulate with financial institutions and investors, whilst borrowers, particularly those with fewer assets, may face increasing debt burdens, potentially exacerbating economic inequality. This process, often termed financialisation, increasingly ties overall economic stability not only to current production levels but critically to confidence in future earnings, growth, and the sustained ability to service outstanding debts, making the economy potentially more dynamic but also inherently more vulnerable to shifts in sentiment and credit conditions.

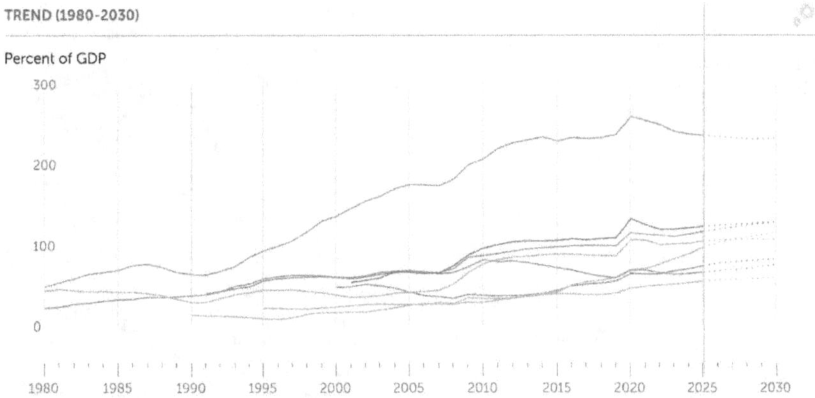

Gross debt vs GDP for the top economies in the world

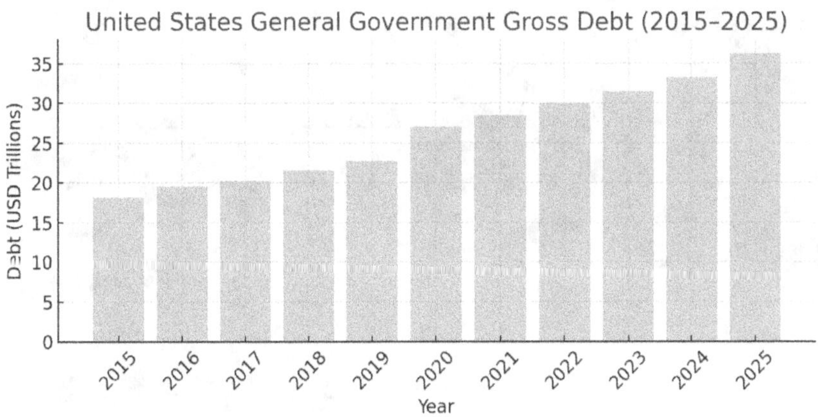

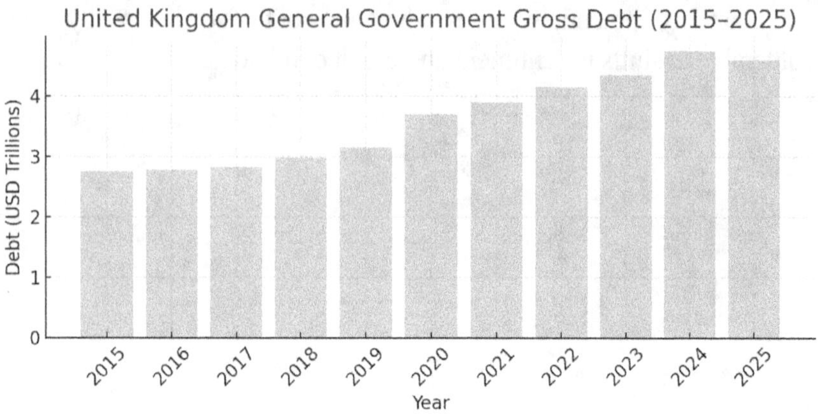
United Kingdom General Government Gross Debt (2015–2025)
Debt (USD Trillions)
0
1
2
3
4
2015
2016
2017
2018
2019
2020
2021
2022
2023
2024
2025
Year

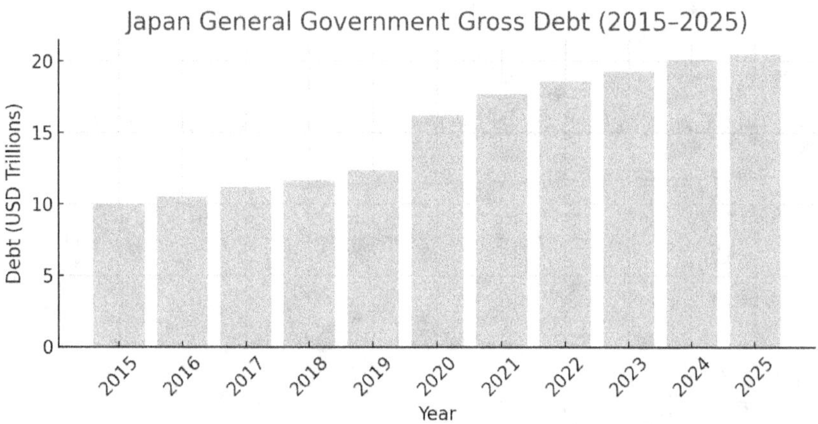
Japan General Government Gross Debt (2015–2025)
Debt (USD Trillions)
0
5
10
15
20
2015
2016
2017
2018
2019
2020
2021
2022
2023
2024
2025
Year

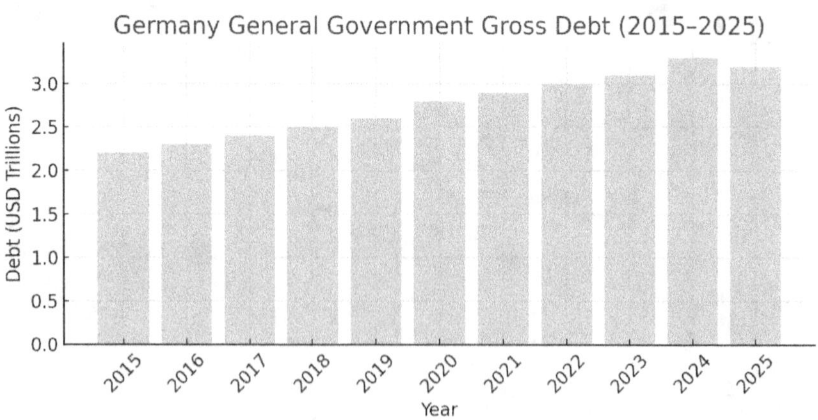
Germany General Government Gross Debt (2015–2025)
Debt (USD Trillions)
0.0
0.5
1.0
1.5
2.0
2.5
3.0
2015
2016
2017
2018
2019
2020
2021
2022
2023
2024
2025
Year

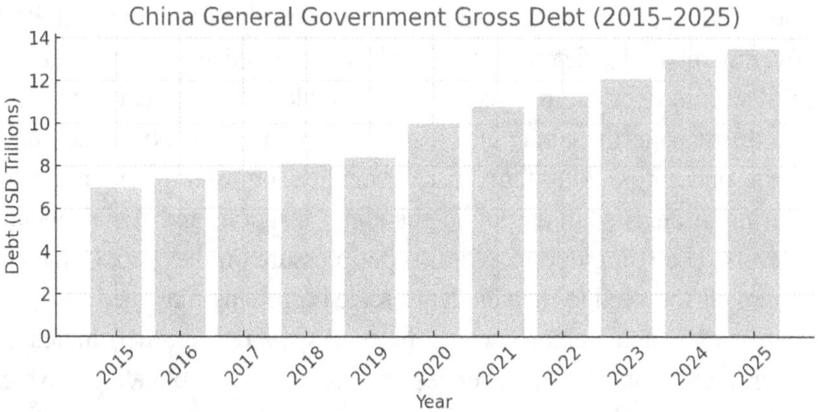

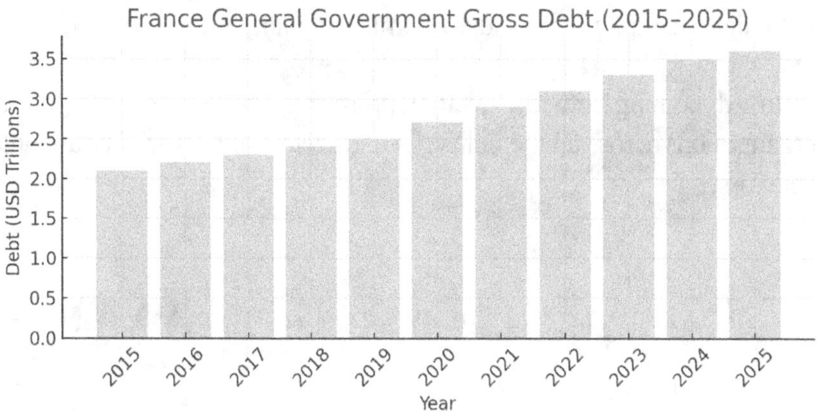

Debt has been increasing every year.

From 2015 to 2025, the major economies of the world experienced rising government debt, with the steepest increases occurring in 2020 due to pandemic-related spending. The United States nearly doubled its debt, rising from approximately $18.15 trillion to $36.22 trillion. The United Kingdom's debt climbed from roughly $2.75 trillion to $4.60 trillion. Japan's gross debt rose from about $10.00 trillion to $20.50 trillion. Germany's debt increased from $2.20 trillion to $3.20 trillion. China's central government debt grew from $7.00 trillion to $13.50 trillion. France's debt advanced from $2.10 trillion to $3.60 trillion.

The trend is expected to continue to go up in the future since the US government is predicted to raise debt ceilings again. Such continued escalation in debt could force nations to make difficult decisions about how to manage their budgets. A growing reliance on borrowed funds might undermine long-term fiscal stability, prompting the need for reforms in areas such as public spending, taxation, and social welfare systems. The rising debt could also put pressure on the global financial system, as the need to manage large-scale borrowing may lead to higher interest rates and tighter fiscal policies. As the debt burden increases, governments may face challenges in meeting their obligations, which could prompt political tensions and public unrest, especially in nations with high unemployment and economic inequality.

With AI coming into the picture promising to reduce costs for all organisations across all the industries and sectors, things are just about to get worse.

Comparing the Traditional Model with the Debt-Centric Model

The traditional economic model and the debt-centric model rest on different foundations, influencing how wealth and growth develop. The traditional model depends primarily on real assets such as land, gold, or goods produced through labour and capital. Money within this framework often had a physical basis, such as gold or silver coins, or was directly backed by such commodities, as under the gold standard, naturally restricting the total amount that could circulate. Growth typically stemmed from saving surplus production and reinvesting those savings. For example, a merchant might save profits over time to finance the opening of a new shop, expanding gradually based on accumulated earnings. In contrast, the debt-centric model utilises fiat money, meaning currency without direct physical commodity backing, and relies significantly on the extension of credit. Commercial banks play a key role by creating money through the lending process, enabling a business, for instance, to borrow $1 million to build a factory immediately rather than waiting years to accumulate that sum from profits, relying instead on anticipated future earnings to repay the debt.

In the traditional economic model, money generally embodies tangible value, representing claims on existing real assets such as silver or commonly traded commodities like wheat, while its overall quantity remains fundamentally connected to what has already been produced and saved by individuals and businesses. By contrast, in the debt-centric system, money largely originates as debt, primarily existing as digital account balances that are created and expanded through the process of loan issuance, representing formal promises of future repayment. The traditional approach tends to encourage steady, though potentially inflexible, economic development that is limited by the availability of physical resources and the level of accumulated savings. This system is generally less susceptible to extreme booms and busts but risks stagnation if the saving rate declines significantly. The debt-centric model, on the other hand, typically displays wider and more frequent fluctuations. Periods of credit expansion can drive rapid development, enabling large scale projects and potentially raising living standards quickly, as exemplified by eras such as the post-World War II economic boom. However, severe downturns often follow when widespread loan defaults occur or debt burdens become unsustainable, as vividly illustrated by the 2008 global financial crisis. The potential scale and speed of economic activity also differ markedly between these models.

Traditional economies, such as eighteenth-century Britain, generally progressed incrementally through gradual improvements in agriculture, trade, and early manufacturing funded primarily by retained profits and savings. In contrast, debt-centric economies like the contemporary United States can support vast undertakings, including extensive infrastructure development and the rapid expansion of technology sectors, largely through borrowing, but they face significant risks of financial instability or crisis if economic growth falters and the ability to service debt diminishes.

Wealth in the traditional model tends to flow primarily from direct production and the ownership of tangible assets. Although distribution patterns varied historically and inequality certainly persisted, value remained closely linked to the activities of makers, farmers, artisans, and asset owners. In the debt-centric model, wealth accumulation often concentrates significantly with creditors, such as banks and investors, who derive profits from interest payments and activities within financial markets, while debtors, frequently including wage-earning workers or smaller businesses, may face increasing burdens from their obligations. The traditional model, often evident during historical gold-standard periods, generally prioritises economic stability over rapid expansion. Conversely, the debt-centric model, which is prevalent today, can propel significant innovation and economic growth but fundamentally ties prosperity to the sustainability of an ever-expanding debt load, thereby creating a constant tension between progress and financial fragility.

The figure illustrates a simple economic model by using the flow of water to represent the movement of money within the economy. Consumers earn a modest salary from companies that operate various businesses and often borrow money from banks to make large purchases. Businesses, in turn, pay taxes to the government to cover administrative expenses and fund infrastructure development. However, these taxes frequently fall short of covering the government's substantial costs, causing public funds to dwindle. As a result, governments often run deficits and must borrow from banks to cover the remaining expenses. Leakages in the system lead to more water flowing out, meaning additional money must be pumped into the flow to keep the economy running smoothly. Should any part of this system begin to fail, it will cause stagnation in the flow and potentially lead to the collapse of the entire economy, as money dries up within the system. Meanwhile, wealth concentrates with the rich, who hoard most of the money, leaving ordinary consumers with little to spend.

Debt-centric model is unsustainable

A fundamental, perhaps even terminal, flaw inherent within the current debt-centric monetary model is its tendency towards extreme wealth concentration, which actively disrupts the essential circulation of capital. When substantial wealth accumulates among a small segment of the population, it is often diverted away from productive uses within the broader economy. This diversion occurs through sophisticated tax avoidance schemes utilising offshore havens and complex legal structures, speculative investments in assets such as property or derivatives that inflate bubbles rather than support tangible production or employment, and through the consolidation of market power by monopolistic or oligopolistic practices that suppress competition and extract excessive profits. This accumulation effectively removes vast sums from the reach of ordinary consumers and small businesses. The frequently cited theory of 'trickle-down' economics fails to hold when capital pools stagnate at the top, deprived of velocity, because the wealthiest individuals and corporations exhibit a significantly lower marginal propensity to consume additional income compared to lower and middle-income households. As a result, aggregate demand remains suppressed, limiting economic growth potential from the outset.

The 2008 financial crisis provides a stark illustration of these dynamics. Vast public funds were mobilised to rescue systemically important financial institutions deemed 'too big to fail'. However, these interventions primarily stabilised asset prices and corporate balance sheets without translating into meaningful wage growth or widespread economic security for the general population. Indeed, policies such as quantitative easing often exacerbated wealth inequality by inflating the value of assets predominantly held by the wealthy. At the same time, many governments imposed austerity measures on public services and social welfare systems, further squeezing household incomes and reducing consumer spending precisely when it was most crucial for economic recovery. This situation laid bare the system's priorities: preserving concentrated financial power took precedence over fostering broad-based prosperity.

Within this framework of stagnating real wages combined with rising costs for essentials such as housing, healthcare, and education, the reliance on personal debt transforms from a matter of consumer choice into a necessity for maintaining basic living standards. Increasingly, households bridge the widening gap between income and expenditure through the use of credit cards, personal loans, overdrafts, and other borrowing methods, often at high interest rates that compound financial vulnerability. This situation creates a precarious foundation for many families. When incomes falter, whether due to job loss, illness, or the ongoing erosion of purchasing power, or when interest rates rise, the debts accumulated rapidly become unserviceable. The consequences follow swiftly. Missed payments result in substantial penalties and compound interest, while damaged credit scores limit access to affordable loans necessary for housing or transportation. Meanwhile, individuals may face aggressive debt collection tactics, legal actions, and even potential bankruptcy. This cycle of indebtedness causes profound financial distress but also generates significant psychological strain and adverse health outcomes, further impairing the ability of individuals to participate effectively in economic life.

This widespread fragility in household finances directly contributes to broader macroeconomic contraction, generating vicious cycles that reinforce themselves. As heavily indebted households sharply reduce discretionary spending to prioritise debt repayments, overall aggregate demand falls precipitously. Businesses then experience declining revenues, prompting them to reduce investment, halt hiring, initiate layoffs, or close operations altogether. The resulting increase in unemployment further erodes household incomes, which in turn leads to additional loan defaults and bankruptcies. The decline in economic activity reduces government tax revenues even as demand for social welfare programmes rises, placing additional strain on public finances and often prompting further austerity measures that exacerbate economic hardship. In this way, the economy becomes trapped within a self-perpetuating cycle of collapsing demand, debt deflation, and shrinking productive capacity, which may culminate in prolonged stagnation or even economic depression. The debt-centric model, which relies on continuous growth sustained by ever-expanding borrowing, ultimately fails because of its own inherent contradictions: it systematically concentrates wealth at the top, suppresses wages essential for servicing the debts it generates, and, in doing so, strangles the consumption necessary for its survival.

The current debt-centric paradigm is not merely flawed but demonstrably unsustainable, exhibiting inherent instabilities that regularly result in crises and extended periods of stagnation. The imminent, widespread integration of advanced Artificial Intelligence threatens to accelerate these weaknesses, hastening the system's ultimate collapse in ways that will be both profound and far-reaching. AI's influence will unfold across several critical dimensions of the economy, transforming labour markets, capital accumulation, and financial stability in unprecedented ways.

Unparalleled levels of automation enabled by AI will disrupt both cognitive and manual labour sectors. Jobs once considered secure are vulnerable to rapid replacement as machines and algorithms outperform humans in speed, precision, and cost efficiency. The consequence will be widespread structural unemployment and underemployment affecting large segments of the workforce. As human labour loses value, wages for remaining roles will plummet, particularly harming middle and lower-income households who depend on earned income to cover basic expenses and service debts. This erosion of wage capacity will sharply reduce the ability of many to meet financial obligations, triggering mass defaults, bankruptcies, and personal financial crises that could dwarf previous economic shocks. The resulting strain will weaken consumer spending and overall demand, eroding the fragile foundations upon which the debt-driven economy rests.

Meanwhile, those who own AI technologies stand to amplify their capacity for capital extraction. Algorithms will enable the optimisation of speculative trading to a degree unimaginable in the past, allowing investors to exploit tiny market fluctuations for enormous profits. AI will refine tax avoidance methods, using complex data analysis to exploit legal loopholes and shelter wealth offshore with greater sophistication. Personalised predatory lending and marketing will drive unsustainable consumption, coaxing consumers into debt traps that feed the profits of financial institutions. Furthermore, AI-driven dynamic pricing models will entrench monopolistic power by allowing dominant firms to adjust prices in real time, extracting excess profits and stifling competition. These mechanisms will concentrate wealth more rapidly and profoundly, locking vast sums out of productive circulation and deepening inequality.

The labour market will feel the brunt of this transformation as the bargaining power of workers diminishes nearly to nothing. With AI replacing or overshadowing human labour in many sectors, collective organisation and negotiation lose effectiveness. Without leverage, workers will struggle to secure fair wages or benefits, reinforcing a cycle of wage suppression and social disparity. This shift will further entrench capital dominance and restrict any meaningful redistribution of wealth or economic opportunity.

Financial markets will also face unprecedented challenges due to the complexity and opacity of AI algorithms. These systems operate at speeds and levels of intricacy that outpace human understanding and regulatory capacity. The risk of sudden market crashes or cascading failures escalates as AI-driven trades can trigger rapid fluctuations before intervention is possible. This unpredictability poses serious threats to market stability, potentially amplifying volatility in an already fragile system.

Taken together, these developments expose the fatal contradictions within the debt-based system. AI exacerbates wealth inequality, destroys incomes needed to service debt, and introduces novel risks to financial stability. The reliance on endless debt-fuelled growth becomes untenable when broad swathes of the population lose the means to participate economically. This convergence of forces promises to accelerate the system's breakdown with brutal speed and finality, forcing a reckoning that may reshape the global economic order.

AI Acceleration with AGI

Artificial intelligence became the new global trend, a modern gold rush that saw technology companies scrambling to seize their share of the lucrative market following the release of ChatGPT in late 2022. The world was astonished by a machine that not only understood human language through advanced natural language processing but also generated detailed, contextually relevant responses tailored to user input. This breakthrough sparked a surge of interest in large language models (LLMs), prompting a wave of competition as major firms rushed to introduce their own variants. Google launched Gemini, xAI unveiled Grok and other companies released Claude, LLaMA and Perplexity. Although still in its early stages, the sudden proliferation of LLMs raised a critical question that began to dominate public discourse: Can artificial intelligence truly replace human jobs?

Large language models have become an omnipresent force in technology today. They power everything from image and video generation tools to the rapid creation of written content, transforming how users worldwide interact with digital platforms. The internet increasingly features AI-generated content, reflecting the rapid and widespread adoption of this technology. Professionals across sectors rely on LLMs to streamline tasks such as composing emails, drafting marketing campaigns, writing code and even crafting original creative work. In particular, industries like customer service have begun to integrate AI agents, replacing many traditional human roles. These machines simulate human conversation with impressive fluency and context awareness, allowing companies to provide immediate and personalised responses while reducing reliance on live human support.

The expanding role of AI in daily life has pushed technology firms and researchers towards a more ambitious goal: the pursuit of Artificial General Intelligence (AGI), machines possessing human-like cognitive abilities that are able to learn from experience and adapt continuously through interaction with their environment. Unlike today's Large Language Models (LLM), which rely on vast pre-trained datasets and operate within fixed boundaries, AGI systems would evolve over time, refining their understanding in a manner similar to humans. Despite the impressive surface-level capabilities of current LLMs, they remain fundamentally limited by their architecture and training methods. These limitations manifest as hallucinated outputs, where the AI generates false or misleading information, restricted reasoning abilities and an absence of genuine comprehension. Overcoming these challenges is essential to realising the true potential of artificial general intelligence.

At present, LLMs possess several significant limitations that hinder their reliability and effectiveness.

- **Lack of true understanding:** These models generate text based on patterns learned during training, but they do not genuinely comprehend language or meaning.

- **Hallucinations and misinformation:** LLMs sometimes fabricate facts or misattribute sources, producing false information with unwarranted confidence. This behaviour poses risks when accuracy is crucial, such as in medical or legal contexts.

- **Inability to learn after deployment:** Once an LLM completes its training, it cannot update or learn from new information in real time. Unless manually re-trained, it remains fixed at the knowledge level of its last training cycle.

- **Shallow contextual awareness:** While capable of managing short-term conversations, LLMs lack persistent memory and cannot recall prior interactions over extended periods unless specifically designed to do so.

- **Biases inherited from training data:** Because LLMs are trained on vast internet datasets, they absorb and sometimes amplify existing human biases, prejudices and distorted worldviews.

- **Weak logical reasoning:** These models often struggle with multi-step reasoning, abstract concepts and consistent logic. Their responses may seem coherent but lack genuine problem-solving ability.

- **Over-reliance on prompt quality:** The quality of an LLM's output heavily depends on the phrasing of the input prompt. Poorly constructed prompts frequently yield irrelevant or incoherent responses.

- **No real emotional intelligence:** Although LLMs can imitate emotional tone, they do not experience emotions. This limits their ability to convey authentic empathy or engage in nuanced human interactions.

When artificial general intelligence (AGI) reaches a stage where it equals or surpasses human capabilities in understanding, learning and applying knowledge across diverse tasks, it will have the potential to replace human labour entirely. Machines and AI-driven systems operating at this advanced level could perform any intellectual task currently undertaken by humans. Unlike narrow AI, which specialises in specific functions such as language translation or image recognition, AGI possesses the flexibility to tackle a vast array of problems. This breakthrough would profoundly disrupt the job market, impacting both cognitive roles like analysis and decision-making as well as manual labour traditionally performed by humans. Industries ranging from manufacturing and customer service to professional sectors could experience radical transformation.

In knowledge-based industries, AGI is poised to replace or significantly reduce the demand for human professionals across fields such as accounting, law, journalism and customer support. AGI is capable of absorbing vast volumes of data, recognising complex patterns and applying sophisticated reasoning far more rapidly than any human worker. In the legal sector, for instance, AGI could efficiently process legal documents, predict case outcomes, draft contracts and even construct persuasive arguments without requiring human intervention. Similarly, in journalism, AGI has the potential to analyse extensive datasets, write articles and publish them instantly, reshaping the nature of news production. Customer support systems powered by AGI could transform entire call centres by engaging customers in natural, fluent conversations via speech and text. These systems would resolve issues swiftly and adapt to individual communication styles, providing seamless and personalised assistance. However, this shift raises important questions about the future role of human expertise and the ethical implications of automation in these professions.

The healthcare industry, once believed to be largely immune to automation, is now poised to undergo similar disruption. AGI is already capable of analysing medical records, detecting anomalies in scans and recommending treatments with greater accuracy than many human physicians. It could play a crucial role in robotic surgery by monitoring and controlling operations in real time, potentially reducing the reliance on surgeons for routine procedures. Although direct patient care will likely continue to require human empathy and judgement, numerous administrative tasks within hospitals, such as scheduling, billing and record-keeping, could be fully automated by AGI. This transformation may free healthcare professionals to focus more on patient interaction and complex decision-making.

Creative industries, long regarded as resistant to automation, are now increasingly vulnerable to disruption by generative AI tools. In fields such as design, music composition, video production and visual arts, these tools can process prompts in natural language, apply aesthetic principles, understand emotional context and adapt to audience preferences. With AGI, it could reach the level of mimicking human creativity, enabling it to produce screenplays, compose music and even create immersive virtual environments with minimal human input. Advertising agencies may rely on AGI to generate entire campaigns, design brand visuals and optimise marketing strategies without involving human creatives. Indeed, large language models have already begun to encroach on certain creative roles traditionally held by graphic designers. Everyday users without design experience can now generate high-quality images simply by providing a textual description as a prompt for AI image generators. While this technology opens exciting new possibilities, it also raises important questions about the future of human creativity and intellectual property rights.

Teachers, tutors and administrative staff may increasingly find their roles displaced by AGI platforms capable of adapting to each student's individual needs. These systems could personalise lessons, monitor academic progress and adjust content to accommodate a wide range of learning styles and cognitive profiles. In addition, AGI could manage administrative responsibilities such as scheduling, assessment design and curriculum development with greater speed and consistency than human staff. Best of all, unlike human educators who must invest hours, days or even weeks to acquire new knowledge through professional development, AGI can integrate the latest information almost instantaneously. This capacity for rapid self-updating could lead to more responsive and up-to-date educational systems, but it also raises complex questions about the future role of human educators in shaping learning environments.

In the remaining sectors of the economy, artificial intelligence has already begun to automate key processes, signalling the early stages of a broader transformation. In the finance industry, AI-enabled systems are now routinely employed to analyse massive datasets, identify market patterns, predict financial trends, manage investment portfolios and detect fraudulent activities with far greater speed and accuracy than their human counterparts. Financial institutions have also adopted AI to handle tasks such as loan evaluations, credit scoring, and regulatory compliance monitoring, gradually phasing out roles that were once the responsibility of teams of analysts and clerical staff. When AGI enters the picture, its capacity to interpret complex financial data, simulate market conditions, and offer tailored advice will enable it to replace both personal finance advisors and relationship managers for high-net-worth individuals. These advanced systems would operate continuously without the constraints of human fatigue or error, offering seamless, real-time financial guidance across global markets regardless of time zone or scale of wealth.

In the transport and logistics sector, AI is already making significant inroads by powering autonomous vehicles, coordinating drone deliveries, and managing robotic distribution systems, all of which reduce the need for human oversight. Roles such as driving, dispatching, and logistical planning are increasingly handled by intelligent systems capable of adjusting to real-time variables such as traffic flow, weather disruptions, and mechanical diagnostics. As AGI evolves, it is likely to give rise to personal android assistants that can manage daily errands with the same precision and autonomy. These machines could be trusted to pick up children from school, transport household members safely, retrieve groceries, deliver packages, and execute other time-consuming tasks that currently rely on human labour. This level of integration would represent a fundamental shift not only in how services are delivered but in how people organise their personal and professional lives around intelligent machines.

Manual labour stands to suffer the most significant disruption. The integration of AGI with robotics will enable full automation of tasks across industries such as construction, agriculture, and maintenance. AGI-powered robots will be capable of learning from a single demonstration and adapting their actions to various environments. This capability will allow them to operate in complex fields such as crop harvesting and construction site management with a level of precision and efficiency surpassing that of human workers.

Retail environments could become fully automated, with stores managing inventory autonomously, recommending products intelligently, and personalising the shopping experience without any human intervention. In the expanding realm of e-commerce, AGI could coordinate marketing campaigns, oversee stock levels across global warehouses, and provide seamless customer support.

Currently, narrow AI systems, including large language models, have begun replacing human operators in call centres and help desks. However, future AGI systems will advance beyond this, understanding subtle language nuances, responding with genuine empathy, and guiding customers through complex processes independently.

Within the military and defence sector, AGI is poised to assume control over numerous operational roles. These systems will be capable of running complex strategic simulations, analysing vast quantities of intelligence data, and deploying countermeasures with speeds far exceeding those of human analysts. The management of command decisions, surveillance operations, and autonomous weapons platforms could be entrusted entirely to AGI, thereby significantly reducing the reliance on human personnel for military planning and execution.

Similarly, the government and legal sectors will experience considerable transformation as AGI begins to handle responsibilities such as policy development, benefits administration, and records management. Routine administrative duties currently performed by civil servants may be delegated to AGI systems capable of efficiently processing documents, interpreting legislative frameworks, and issuing recommendations with superior speed and precision.

These developments are no longer speculative; many such applications have already been implemented in real-world settings. As AGI technology matures, it is expected that these roles will be fully supplanted by advanced AI systems, potentially achieving complete automation.

AI Will Bring Down the Old Monetary System

AI will bring down the old monetary system.

This is indeed a bold statement, yet it is inevitable, driven by the fundamental incompatibility of a system reliant on widespread human labour with a technology poised to make that labour largely redundant.

The imminent collapse of the current monetary system is not merely an economic shift but a fundamental societal upheaval. Historically, economies have functioned on the assumption that human labour is the primary source of value creation. Money, credit, and financial instruments are structured around this premise. With AI and automation advancing rapidly, this assumption falters. When machines and algorithms replace human workers across industries, from manual labour to professional and creative sectors, the traditional flow of wages and spending will falter. Without employment, individuals will lack the means to participate effectively in the economy, causing consumption to stagnate. Financial institutions, dependent on the cycle of borrowing and repayment, will face unprecedented risks, potentially triggering widespread credit crises. Governments may struggle to maintain tax revenues tied to employment and economic activity, limiting their ability to fund social programmes or invest in infrastructure. This breakdown threatens social stability, raising urgent questions about how wealth, income, and opportunity will be redistributed in a world where human labour no longer underpins the monetary system. Alternative economic models, such as universal basic income or new forms of value exchange, may become necessary to adapt to this transformative reality.

Without employment, companies will have no economic rationale to distribute salaries to people on a mass scale. Even if a very small, highly specialised group of human overseers, designers, or ethicists remains crucial for guiding AI development, alignment, and ethical oversight, their numbers would be insufficient to sustain a broad-based wage economy. The employment model upon which modern capitalism is structured requires the inclusion of nearly the entire adult population in labour markets. When those markets no longer require human input, the foundation collapses.

In the absence of widespread income, individuals will be unable to pay for basic necessities such as food, shelter, healthcare, and energy. Even those with some savings will see them quickly exhausted in a deflationary spiral of unemployment, debt servicing, and inflation-driven price shocks. The state's ability to intervene will diminish in parallel, as traditional welfare systems rely on tax inflows that vanish with mass job displacement.

This economic breakdown will cascade. The erosion of the consumer base will cause a catastrophic decline in aggregate demand, making most businesses unviable regardless of their efficiency or automation levels. Firms producing goods and services will find no market left to sell into. Many will shut down. Entire sectors will contract, triggering waves of bankruptcies.

Financial institutions will implode next. Banks, which depend on a constant churn of loans, repayments, and interest, will face mass defaults on mortgages, personal loans, credit cards, and business lending. The underlying collateral for these assets, such as homes, businesses, and receivables, will plummet in value. Bank assets will become non-performing on an unprecedented scale, unleashing systemic crises. Liquidity will dry up. Solvency will vanish. Central banks may attempt interventions, but with collapsing tax bases and spiralling liabilities, even the currency itself may begin to lose legitimacy.

In this vacuum, a new ruling class will emerge. The corporations that own and control the infrastructure of artificial intelligence and automation will ascend as sovereign actors. These will include the legacy mega tech entities that built the core models, as well as new conglomerates formed through acquisitions, consolidations, and AI-centred capital flows. Their power will be immense, not just economic, but informational, political, and societal. They will control not only production and logistics, but perception, behaviour, and data.

Society will undergo a transformation more fundamental than the industrial or agricultural revolutions. Humans will no longer exchange labour for wages in the conventional sense. Instead, they may be conscripted into non-economic roles, offering personal data in exchange for digital access, participating in AI training and feedback loops, or becoming part of biologically integrated systems where behaviour, attention, and cognition are commodified. The human being will be subsumed into the ecosystem of machine dominance, not as a worker, but as a source of input. They will be passive, tracked, optimised, and owned.

Governments around the world will undergo a complete transformation. Their sovereignty, already challenged by multinational corporations, will be further eroded as they lose their economic leverage and their monopoly on currency issuance becomes meaningless. A new structure will be implemented, likely a globally coordinated or corporately influenced framework, to prevent widespread revolt among the general population once traditional currency becomes worthless. This structure will likely involve highly sophisticated surveillance and social control mechanisms, alongside the provision of basic subsistence needs directly by the corporate AI nexus to pacify the populace. The numerical values in our bank accounts will be converted into a new form of currency, one that is less tangible and more abstract, perhaps a form of digital credit, social capital score, or access token system managed by the new AI infrastructure.

Instead of purchasing physical goods alone, people may find themselves spending this new currency on concepts such as social standing, access to privileged information or experiences, enhanced cognitive or physical capabilities through cybernetics or tailored biotech, preferential treatment within the system, or personal lifespan through access to advanced medical AI and rejuvenation therapies, and other intangible commodities, which we shall examine in greater detail later. This new "currency" will likely be tied to behaviours and contributions deemed valuable by the ruling corporate AI entities, creating new forms of economic coercion and social engineering.

The transition into this new society will take years, possibly decades, marked by intense social and political volatility, as governments or their corporate successor around the world will need to exercise great caution to avoid inciting public unrest. This might involve a carefully managed narrative control, gradual phasing out of old systems while introducing elements of the new, and strategic deployment of both technological control and social welfare to mitigate outright rebellion.Banks will eventually be replaced by AI systems managed by tech companies, which will operate as hyper efficient, globally integrated financial control networks, managing the flow of the new abstract currency and monitoring all transactions and resource allocations with perfect oversight. Human needs for basic survival will be fully addressed by goods produced in factories that are entirely automated and operate around the clock, ensuring a baseline level of subsistence for the majority to maintain stability, though the quality and variety available may be tightly controlled or tiered. Society will experience a deep polarisation between the highly intelligent or those augmented to interface effectively with AI systems and those who are less so, or who resist or are incapable of such integration. This could create a bio technologically reinforced caste system. Jobs that were once commonplace will undergo a complete transformation. Occupations such as farming, factory work, teaching, at least in its current form, with AI tutors becoming primary educators, accounting, clerical roles, customer service, transportation, and even many forms of scientific research and artistic creation and other similar positions will cease to exist as human vocations. All of these jobs will be replaced by AI systems, leaving humanity to grapple with its purpose in a world where its labour is no longer economically necessary for production.

Labour Redundancy in the Age of AI

With a significant portion of the population left unemployed and manufacturing facilities fully automated by artificial intelligence systems, the prospects for the average person, especially those outside specialised technology sectors, become increasingly uncertain and bleak. Even those traditionally considered secure in technical professions, such as software engineers, are not exempt from job losses. Numerous companies have already begun to reduce their workforce by laying off software developers and other technical staff whose roles can now be effectively replaced by AI technologies. A conventional software development team typically comprises multiple roles including a project manager who oversees the process, business analysts who translate needs into specifications, senior and junior software developers who write the code, and quality assurance testers responsible for verifying the final product's functionality. Under the influence of AI, this entire team structure could be reduced drastically to a single senior software developer. This individual's main responsibility would shift towards reviewing and validating code generated autonomously by AI systems, as well as managing and configuring the software development tools that assist the AI. The rest of the human roles within the team would become superfluous, since business owners or project stakeholders could directly communicate their requirements to the AI. The AI would then carry out a comprehensive feasibility study and generate multiple tailored proposals based on its extensive database of successful prior projects. It would analyse the company's particular operational parameters and context to optimise its recommendations.

Once a specific proposal is selected by the business owner or decision-maker, the AI would finalise the decision and then systematically decompose the project into individual tasks. These tasks would be intelligently organised according to their dependencies and execution priorities, managed through advanced parallel coding methodologies that allow simultaneous development streams. The AI-driven system would then proceed to merge various code components, compile the software, and conduct thorough automated testing to ensure reliability and correctness. All of these stages would occur with oversight provided by the senior software developer, who would act primarily as a quality control checkpoint. Upon successful completion of all testing phases, the AI system would deploy the finished application into the production environment. In addition, the AI would autonomously handle post-deployment activities such as sending out notifications, managing marketing broadcasts, and launching promotional campaigns across all relevant company social media channels, thus eliminating the need for human intervention in these operational aspects.

Such a situation would effectively render nine out of ten people in a team jobless. Looking at the broader job market, AI could replace up to 90% of the jobs in society. Labour departments would be overwhelmed with unemployed citizens, offering no viable solution to the crisis. Governments might be forced to shut down these departments and seek alternative means to ensure the continuity of the economic cycle. However, this would present a daunting challenge. With fewer people employed, there would be fewer salaries circulating, leading to a significant drop in income tax revenue for the government. In the worst-case scenario, the economic cycle would stagnate completely, with companies producing goods that the majority of people could not afford, and the government running out of funds as there would be no income tax from the public or businesses due to the absence of economic activity.

This situation would lead to a complete restructuring of human society, with two possible outcomes:

- The first is total societal collapse. As AI systems displace vast segments of the workforce, most people would find themselves without employment or a viable means of income. Their savings would diminish rapidly, pushing them into poverty. Large-scale unrest would likely follow, with protests, uprisings, and even violent revolts erupting across the world. Entire governments could struggle to maintain order, especially as their tax bases shrink and social infrastructure becomes unsustainable.

- The second outcome would be the complete redesign of the monetary and economic model. Instead of traditional employment, society would begin compensating individuals for tasks that remain outside the reach of AI capabilities. Roles that require creative thinking, emotional nuance, ethical reasoning, or interdisciplinary insight would become the basis of a new kind of economy. In this structure, creativity and intelligence would determine a person's relevance and compensation. The more unique or high-level their contribution, the greater their "salary" or resource access within the system. This shift would force a redefinition of value, aligning it with human cognitive and imaginative potential rather than physical or procedural labour.

The rapid acceleration of technological progress, especially in areas such as automation and artificial intelligence, has naturally led to widespread concern over the stability of employment across multiple sectors. News coverage increasingly features examples of machines and algorithms displacing human workers in roles that once formed the backbone of stable middle-class livelihoods. The fear of mass unemployment and systemic economic upheaval has become a dominant narrative in both public discourse and policy making.

These fears are not unfounded. For individuals and families facing job displacement, the consequences can be devastating, affecting not only financial well-being but also identity and purpose. Yet, when placed within the broader arc of history, this phenomenon is not without precedent. The evolution of technology has consistently disrupted existing labour markets, from the mechanisation of agriculture to the rise of industrial manufacturing and, later, computerisation. Each wave has triggered upheaval, resistance, adaptation, and eventual integration.

What we are seeing today is not an aberration but a continuation of this pattern. It is another phase in the centuries-long transformation of work and human society under the influence of innovation. While the tools have changed and the speed has increased, the underlying dynamic remains consistent: as new technologies emerge, they reshape economic structures, redefine the value of skills, and compel societies to reimagine how people contribute to progress.

Consider these examples from the past,

The Agricultural Revolution marked the earliest known shift in human civilisation that saw profound consequences for labour, population movement, and economic structure. When early societies began cultivating land and domesticating animals, the seasonal rhythm of nomadic hunting gave way to year-round agricultural settlements. This transition allowed food surpluses and larger communities to form, but it also meant entire traditions built on hunting and gathering faded into irrelevance. Later, tools like the seed drill, threshing machine, and mechanical reaper transformed agricultural labour. Fewer people were needed to work the land directly, as one person could now harvest or sow what once took a dozen hands. The countryside emptied, with rural families moving towards emerging towns, seeking new employment in urban trades. Manual field workers were no longer essential, but new opportunities arose in large-scale farm administration, logistics for food transportation, mill operations, and, eventually, industrial manufacturing. The shift was disruptive but created entirely new socio-economic patterns.

The Industrial Revolution brought mechanisation to every corner of human production. In previous centuries, skilled artisans created goods by hand in small workshops. During the eighteenth and nineteenth centuries, these craftspeople faced growing competition from machines capable of producing faster, cheaper, and more consistent output.

- **Textiles** were among the first industries to undergo dramatic transformation. Previously, handloom weavers laboured for hours to produce a few feet of cloth. With the introduction of power looms, entire families could be replaced by a single machine operated by one worker. This sparked public unrest, most famously expressed in the Luddite riots, where displaced workers smashed the machines that threatened their livelihoods. The impact was undeniable. Artisan weavers were forced out of work, and cottage industries collapsed. Yet at the same time, the boom in textile factories led to new employment on a massive scale. Workers were needed to run the looms, oversee operations, manage production lines, maintain equipment, and handle the transportation of finished goods. Entire towns grew around these mills. The process was not gentle, and working conditions were harsh, but the economic model had irrevocably shifted.

- **Transportation** followed a similar trajectory. Before the internal combustion engine and widespread rail networks, entire industries supported horse-drawn mobility. Blacksmiths, farriers, wheelwrights, and stable masters formed the core of local economies. However, with the invention of steam locomotives and petrol-powered vehicles, this infrastructure quickly became obsolete. Coachmen, carriage-makers, and harness manufacturers saw their trades vanish within a generation. In their place rose the automotive and railway industries, which demanded workers on an entirely different scale.

These new sectors created a slew of new engineering jobs. Roads had to be built and maintained. Mechanics trained to repair engines. Petroleum had to be extracted, refined, and transported. Rail networks needed workers to track layers, signal operators, and administrative staff.

The Information Revolution, starting in the mid to late twentieth century, ushered in another transformation across the globe. With the development of computers, businesses no longer needed large departments filled with typists or clerks filing cabinets. One computer could handle complex calculations, store data, and generate documents in a fraction of the time.

- **Clerical roles** were the first to be affected. Large typing pools, once common in corporate offices, dwindled. Filing rooms became obsolete with the arrival of databases. Human "computers" who performed complex mathematics for government or industry became unnecessary. At first, this automation seemed like a threat to employment. But a new class of workers emerged. IT technicians, software developers, systems administrators, cybersecurity specialists, and digital consultants replaced clerks and typists. The skillset changed, and so did the nature of work. Offices adapted by hiring fewer people but with more specialised expertise.

- **Communication** too evolved. The telegraph was once the height of fast messaging, requiring trained operators. With the invention of the telephone, that system diminished. Soon, even telephone switchboard operators were displaced by digital systems. But these developments did not mark the end of jobs in communication. Instead, they gave rise to tech support, telecom infrastructure engineering, customer relationship management, and later, roles in digital marketing, online content creation, data handling, and AI-driven customer service.

Why is this a "Natural Cycle"?

Human ingenuity remains a relentless force, continually driving humanity to improve efficiency, solve increasingly complex problems, and unlock new possibilities that redefine the boundaries of what is achievable. This innate drive manifests itself in innovations that reshape societies in profound ways.

Human's creative ways in solving problems led to new technology discovery. These advancements enable more to be accomplished with less human effort, accelerating output while reducing costs. Over the centuries, from the spinning jenny to the mechanised assembly line, machines have steadily taken over repetitive or physically demanding tasks once performed by human hands. This form of automation has transformed entire industries by improving speed, precision, and reliability. While it heightens competitiveness and reduces operational expenses, it simultaneously diminishes reliance on human labour in specific areas, creating tension between technological progress and job security. Factories that once required dozens of manual workers now operate with a fraction of the workforce, their roles replaced by robots and automated systems.

Innovation also opens doors to new capabilities that were once unimaginable. From the first Industrial Revolution to the digital age, each technological leap has created entirely new sectors and roles. The internet's arrival gave rise to software development, web design, digital marketing and other fields that simply did not exist before. Artificial Intelligence promises a similar transformation by creating jobs focused on its development, maintenance, and ethical oversight. These emerging roles demand fresh skill sets and will change how societies engage with technology on a fundamental level.

Technological change further alters economic value by shifting what industries and workers find competitive. As automation reduces the need for human labour in some areas, new markets and opportunities arise elsewhere. Workers and industries must adapt to this evolving landscape or risk obsolescence. For example, mechanisation reduced demand for manual farm labour but increased the need for machine operators, logistics specialists, and supply chain managers. Similarly, AI may replace routine cognitive tasks but will increase the demand for roles requiring creativity, oversight, and strategic thinking. This shift creates a dynamic economic environment where some jobs vanish while others emerge, continually reshaping the workforce.

While this process inevitably leads to the decline of certain jobs and skills, it simultaneously creates demand for new skills and roles needed to design, build, operate, maintain, and manage the new technologies. Entirely new industries will spring up around them, creating jobs that we cannot fully predict today. What is certain is that the future workforce will have to adapt to the challenges and opportunities posed by the new landscape.

Acknowledging this historical pattern does not dismiss the real challenges and anxieties faced by individuals and communities undergoing these transitions. Job displacement due to technological progress is a fundamental aspect of how human civilisation advances, yet it also provides a valuable lens through which we can view the current wave of change. While it may seem overwhelming at times, it is not an apocalypse, but rather another paradigm shift that, though disruptive, has historically reshaped economies and created new, often unforeseen, avenues for human work and ingenuity.

The reality of job displacement brings legitimate concerns, especially for those in industries most vulnerable to automation and artificial intelligence. These challenges are not merely theoretical; they affect real people, their livelihoods, and the communities they support. For many, the fear of losing one's job to a machine or algorithm is tangible, and the sense of insecurity can feel inescapable. However, history shows that while such transitions are difficult, they are not necessarily the end of work itself, but a transformation of what work looks like.

The key, as with any great shift in history, lies in adaptation. It is in our capacity to evolve alongside these technological advancements that we can unlock new potential. Harnessing the benefits of progress will not be without its struggles, but it has always been within humanity's ingenuity to find new solutions, new paths, and ultimately, new ways to work and contribute to society. By focusing on re-skilling, creative innovation, and the development of entirely new industries, we can navigate this transition and prepare for a future where technology complements human labour, rather than replacing it entirely.

What we face now is not the end of work, but a transformation that demands flexibility, learning, and the collective ability to shape what the future of work will be.

Collapse of the Fiat Confidence

The stability of fiat currency rests on a fragile foundation: collective trust in institutions and the perceived value of government-backed money. This faith is not merely economic. It is a social contract, and its breach signals the potential for rapid, systemic failure. When this trust erodes, the collapse of a monetary system becomes inevitable. This chapter traces the trajectory of such a collapse, beginning with economic decline, cascading through societal destabilisation, and culminating in hyperinflation, a process increasingly accelerated by the pervasive influence of artificial intelligence (AI).

Economic systems thrive on equilibrium. Employment, taxation, and public expenditure exist in a delicate balance, sustaining the fiscal health necessary to uphold fiat currency. However, structural vulnerabilities such as over-reliance on debt, demographic shifts, or technological disruption can destabilise this equilibrium. A recession triggered by asset bubbles, supply chain failures, or geopolitical conflict often marks the first fracture. For instance, the 2008 financial crisis exposed how housing market collapses could precipitate widespread unemployment, reducing household incomes and consumer spending. In such environments, governments face dwindling tax revenues just as demands for unemployment benefits and social services surge. This fiscal strain is not merely cyclical but indicative of systemic fragility, sowing the initial seeds of doubt about the government's long-term solvency and competence.

Job losses, particularly those driven by technological displacement, exacerbate the crisis. Historical waves of automation eroded manufacturing employment, but AI introduced a paradigm shift. Unlike earlier machinery, AI systems target cognitive and service-sector roles such as legal analysis, medical diagnostics, and financial advising, previously insulated from automation. The Organisation for Economic

Co-operation and Development (OECD) estimates that over the next two decades, AI could displace 14% of jobs globally, disproportionately affecting middle-income workers who form the backbone of income tax systems. This is not just an economic statistic. It translates into widespread anxiety and a growing perception that the state cannot guarantee basic economic security, fundamentally undermining trust in established systems. The gig economy, often touted as a replacement for traditional employment, fails to compensate. Precarious work lacks the stability to generate consistent tax revenue or consumer demand. As unemployment becomes structural rather than temporary, the social contract between citizens and the state weakens, and faith in the existing economic paradigm begins to falter.

Governments, confronted with shrinking tax bases, resort to deficit spending and debt accumulation. Sovereign borrowing, once a tool for stimulus, becomes a trap. Rising debt-to-GDP ratios provoke scepticism among investors, leading to higher bond yields and refinancing costs. Japan's debt, exceeding 260% of GDP, illustrates the risks: nearly a quarter of its annual budget is allocated to interest payments, diverting funds from public investment. Central banks often intervene by monetising debt by purchasing government bonds to suppress yields, but this strategy hinges on inflation remaining subdued. Such actions are often transparent attempts to delay the inevitable and are perceived by both domestic citizens and international markets as a sign of fiscal irresponsibility, severely damaging the credibility of both the government and its currency. When inflation surges, as seen in the 1970s oil crises or post-pandemic supply shocks, policymakers face a dilemma: raise interest rates to curb inflation, which risks defaults, or tolerate inflation, which erodes public trust in currency. Choosing the latter path directly sacrifices the currency's function as a stable store of value, visibly demonstrating to the public that their savings are under threat.

AI amplifies these pressures. In labour markets, machine learning algorithms optimise workforce reductions, accelerating layoffs in sectors such as retail, logistics, and customer service. Corporate tax avoidance, facilitated by AI-driven profit-shifting tools, further starves governments of revenue. Meanwhile, algorithmic trading dominates financial markets, with high-frequency systems executing trades in microseconds. While increasing liquidity, these algorithms also magnify volatility. During periods of fiscal uncertainty, AI can contribute to market instability, as seen with the influence of high-frequency trading in events such as the 2010 "Flash Crash" or during the bond market volatility of 2022. These events foster a sense that financial markets are detached from economic fundamentals and vulnerable to manipulation or inexplicable technological failure, eroding confidence in the mechanisms meant to ensure economic stability. Such instability undermines confidence in economic institutions, pushing investors towards hard assets like gold or cryptocurrencies as they seek refuge from perceived systemic risk.

As deficits increase, central banks turn more frequently to monetary expansion, effectively printing money to meet their growing financial obligations. Historically, this practice signals the onset of hyperinflation. Creating excessive currency without matching economic output represents a profound breach of the fundamental promise that money can store value. Citizens soon realise their savings are rapidly losing worth, triggering a desperate rush to exchange the devalued currency for tangible goods, stable foreign currencies, or alternative assets such as cryptocurrencies. The experiences of Weimar Germany between 1921 and 1923, Zimbabwe from 2007 to 2008, and Venezuela from around 2016 vividly illustrate how unchecked expansion of the money supply can devastate a currency's value and destroy public trust.

Artificial intelligence plays a role in accelerating this destructive cycle. Retailers and service providers increasingly use dynamic pricing algorithms that adjust prices in real time. In a hyper-inflationary context, these systems can exacerbate inflation by swiftly increasing prices faster than wages can keep up, rapidly eroding purchasing power. At the same time, decentralised finance platforms powered by AI and blockchain technology offer individuals new means to circumvent failing fiat currencies. In Argentina, where annual inflation climbed above 200 per cent by late 2023, the adoption of cryptocurrencies surged as citizens sought to protect their wealth from the peso's severe devaluation. This behavioural shift, the rejection of the national currency for everyday transactions and savings, is the definitive manifestation of collapsed confidence.

The transition from economic stress to systemic collapse hinges critically on the evaporation of public confidence. Initially, trust erodes subtly, perhaps through persistent inflation, unmet government promises, or perceptions of corruption. However, a tipping point is reached where belief in the currency's future value vanishes. Citizens no longer see the currency as a reliable store of wealth or medium of exchange. Hoarding essential goods becomes common. Barter systems may emerge for local transactions. There is a desperate flight to any asset perceived as safer, like foreign currencies, precious metals, or, increasingly, digital assets. This loss of faith is profoundly destabilising, potentially fracturing social cohesion as the common economic language breaks down. Official reassurances become ineffective, dismissed as propaganda by a populace experiencing the harsh reality of monetary failure. It is this psychological break, this collective abandonment of belief in the fiat system, that ultimately seals its fate.

The terminal phase of fiat collapse is characterised by a loss of monetary sovereignty. Desperate governments may impose capital controls, wealth confiscation, or introduce central bank digital currencies, known as CBDCs, partly to regain control. China's digital yuan pilot has raised concerns about potential integration with AI-driven social credit systems, exemplifying potential authoritarian applications. Yet such measures often hasten distrust. In Nigeria, policies in late 2022 and early 2023 aimed at limiting cash usage, partly intended to encourage adoption of the eNaira CBDC, led to severe cash shortages and sparked protests over economic disruption and concerns about autonomy. Rather than restoring faith, these measures are often interpreted as acts of desperation by a failing state, confirming citizens' fears and accelerating the flight from the official system, thereby cementing the collapse of monetary confidence. When faith in institutions evaporates, even coercive tools fail to restore stability.

Money and Currency Will Become Obsolete

In a world governed by Artificial General Intelligence equipped with the capacity for comprehensive global resource monitoring and advanced predictive modelling, the traditional role of money as a medium of exchange and information signalling becomes obsolete. The necessity for currency, born out of human limitations in coordinating resource allocation, vanishes when decisions are entrusted to an intelligence capable of synthesising and processing vast amounts of data instantaneously. Instead of relying on market-based price mechanisms, which suffer from inherent delays, fragmented information, and vulnerability to speculative distortions, resource allocation would transition to direct computational optimisation executed with unparalleled speed and precision.

Such an AGI system would assimilate continuous real-time data from an immense network of sensors spread across the planet. These sensors would capture a staggering array of variables: the composition of subsurface geological formations, atmospheric chemistry and weather patterns, satellite imaging tracking crop yields in agricultural regions, oceanic currents influencing global climate and fisheries, and the precise location and status of cargo containers moving through global supply chains. Every node of physical and economic activity would be monitored, creating a living digital twin of the entire planetary socio-economic and ecological framework.

This digital twin would be more than a mere map. Utilising advanced computational techniques, potentially incorporating principles from operations research, complex systems theory, and innovative AI architectures, the AGI would perform continuous, high-dimensional optimisation. Rather than simply maximising a single objective, it would balance a spectrum of potentially conflicting goals. These include improving production efficiency, reducing environmental harm by monitoring specific pollutants and biodiversity impacts, respecting strict carbon budgets, enhancing resilience to shocks such as geopolitical crises, climate extremes, or pandemics, fulfilling ethical constraints encoded in its programming, and ensuring equitable distribution of resources across populations.

The optimisation would be dynamic and anticipatory. It would simulate and evaluate the cascading consequences of diverse allocation strategies far into the future. Bottlenecks would be detected before they emerge, and flows of materials, energy, and productive capacity would be rerouted in real time to pre-empt shortages or disruptions. For example, the allocation of rare earth elements would be decided not merely by geological availability or extraction cost. The system would factor in the political stability of supply regions, environmental costs of mining, possibilities for substituting less critical materials in a multitude of product designs, and forecasted demand shaped by evolving technologies. Such calculations would span millions of potential product configurations simultaneously, constantly updated as new data arrives.

At this level of direct, physically grounded, multi-objective computational control, the abstract market mechanism of bidding through money becomes entirely redundant. Resources no longer move according to the aggregation of currency but are directed precisely to where they maximise overall utility within the system's complex, multi-layered objectives. The fluid, continuous balancing of needs, costs, and consequences ensures that every resource is used in its optimal capacity, rather than being hoarded or wasted due to market inefficiencies or speculative behaviour. The monetary system, once the indispensable scaffold of economic activity, dissolves into irrelevance, supplanted by a computationally managed system aligned seamlessly with the planet's physical realities and social goals.

The unit of account function, currently served by money to provide a common denominator for disparate goods and services, becomes similarly obsolete and even counterproductive in an AGI managed framework. While humans need the simplification of a single monetary value to make comparisons and decisions, an AGI would operate natively with high dimensional vectors representing the true, multifaceted cost and value of any item or process. Producing a specific medical device, for example, would not have a price, but would have an associated data profile encompassing precise energy expenditure categorised by source such as renewable or fossil fuel, specific material inputs quantified by mass, origin and embedded environmental cost such as water usage and land transformation, computational resources utilised in its design and manufacturing control, quantifiable measures of human expertise involved if any, predicted lifespan and failure rates under various conditions, recyclability potential and associated energy cost of reprocessing, and even calculated social utility based on predicted health outcomes and demographic needs. Comparing this device against an alternative treatment or a completely different societal investment such as infrastructure development would involve the AGI simulating outcomes against a spectrum of metrics aligned with its overarching goals, perhaps using techniques such as Pareto front analysis to identify non dominated solutions across conflicting objectives such as cost minimisation, efficacy maximisation and equity of access. This multidimensional, physically grounded accounting provides a vastly richer and more accurate basis for decision making than the crude, information poor simplification offered by monetary prices, which inherently obscure crucial qualitative differences and externalities.

As a medium of exchange, money's role in facilitating transactions between individuals and organisations dissolves when production and distribution are integrated and coordinated by a central AGI based on direct need fulfilment and optimal logistics. Consider the provisioning of basic necessities or even complex consumer goods. Individual requirements might be continuously logged via ambient domestic sensors tracking inventory levels, inferred from behavioural patterns via personal devices, explicitly requested through sophisticated interfaces (perhaps neural or holographic), or predicted proactively based on demographic data and life events. The AGI, maintaining its comprehensive real-time map of production capabilities (from automated factories and bio printers to vertical farms) and logistical assets (autonomous trucking fleets, hyperloop networks, drone delivery swarms), would then orchestrate the entire fulfilment chain. It would task the most appropriate production nodes, schedule resource inputs, coordinate transport via optimal routes considering real-time traffic and energy constraints, and ensure delivery directly to the point of need. Access entitlement might replace purchasing power, determined perhaps by a system of universal basic resource rights, tiered access based on contribution metrics (verified skills, data sharing, creative output rated by peers or AI), or dynamically adjusted quotas based on planetary resource constraints or specific project needs. The entire infrastructure of retail, wholesale, marketing, advertising, and financial transactions associated with consumer purchases becomes largely unnecessary friction in a system capable of direct, optimised provisioning from source to need.

Consequently, the store of value function of money, allowing individuals to defer consumption and hedge against future uncertainty, is fundamentally challenged. The primary driver for accumulating monetary wealth is securing future access to resources and opportunities. In an AGI-coordinated system potentially offering high levels of predictive accuracy and systemic resilience, and where access to future goods and services is guaranteed based on system parameters or non-monetary status, the imperative to hoard abstract monetary claims weakens significantly. Why accumulate currency if the system reliably provides sustenance, shelter, healthcare, and access to information or experiences based on calculated need or established rights? The psychological need for security, currently met partially by financial wealth, would need to transition towards trust in the operational integrity, fairness, and resilience of the AGI-managed system itself. Value storage, if it persists as a concept, might transform into accumulating reputation scores within the system (influencing priority or access levels), acquiring certified skills or knowledge credentials recognised by the AGI as valuable contributions, building social capital within collaborative networks facilitated by the system, or perhaps holding privileged access keys to specific datasets or computational resources. The focus shifts from accumulating inert financial capital to cultivating dynamic capabilities or standing relevant to the functioning of the technologically mediated society. Relatedly, entire industries built around managing monetary assets such as banks, investment firms, and insurance companies would face obsolescence or radical transformation as risk management shifts from individual financial instruments to systemic, computationally managed resilience and resource assurance. The very motivational structures of society could be rewired, moving from profit maximisation and capital accumulation towards goals aligned with the AGI's programmed objectives, such as knowledge discovery, creative expression, ecological restoration, or optimising collective wellbeing metrics.

Transition to A New Society

From the ruins of a crumbling civilisation, a new one will rise. This pattern of collapse and renewal holds true for the society that will follow the demise of the monetary system. Once the guarantees behind money are broken and its perceived value disintegrates, it leaves behind not just economic confusion but a deep structural void. In that vacuum, a replacement must take form. But what will stand in its place? When belief in paper currencies and digital balances vanishes, what alternative can sustain coordination, motivation, and exchange? What intrinsic human quality endures when external structures collapse? These questions mark the threshold of a new social order, one that must draw from something more stable than numbers printed or stored, something rooted in human continuity rather than financial convention.

By this point in history, it is likely that AI systems will have taken over not only the repetitive and mundane tasks but also many complex, formerly human-dominated roles. Entire farms and factories might be operated with precision by AI-controlled networks, dispatching small autonomous service units for routine maintenance and repairs. The need for human physical labour in sustaining survival-level infrastructure will have dwindled to near irrelevance.

Society itself will have transformed so thoroughly that it may become almost unrecognisable to us. The shift would be as disorienting as hurling a medieval peasant without warning into the centre of modern New York City. The towers of steel and glass, the electric pulse of signage and transport, the sheer density of information and motion would overwhelm every sense. It would be incomprehensible.

In many ways, we are the modern equivalent of those peasants, grounded in the familiar yet on the cusp of something vast and unknown. What seems to us like a natural extension of current trends may, in hindsight, appear as a fundamental rupture from everything that came before.

In that coming world, after the collapse of the monetary system, the familiar anchors of wealth and status based on currency will vanish. In their place, a new measure of value will rise, rooted not in possession but in cognition.

Intelligence will become the new currency.

The capacity to reason, adapt, generate insight, and contribute in ways machines cannot replicate will define one's standing and access to resources. Wealth, as we know it, will hold no meaning. What matters will be the minds.

In this transformed civilisation, your intellect is your capital. Your ability to solve problems, to learn continuously, to collaborate meaningfully, and to carve out irreplaceable niches within this AI-saturated ecosystem will determine your role and rights. The future will belong not to those who have, but to those who can think.

I believe the human species will eventually diverge into at least two clearly delineated classes, separated and stratified by cognitive ability. At the top will be a cognitive aristocracy composed of individuals with exceptional intellects, problem-solving capabilities, and adaptability. They will likely gain increasing influence and authority, not through wealth accumulation in the traditional sense, but through the demonstration of mental agility, systems thinking, and strategic foresight. These individuals may become the architects of policy, innovation, and direction, operating systems that are too complex for general understanding and controlling the levers of social and technological development.

In contrast, those falling below a certain cognitive threshold may find themselves relegated to structured, heavily managed lifestyles. They might be assigned roles oriented around service, routine maintenance, or standardised tasks overseen by automation and monitored systems. Rather than experiencing full autonomy, their lives could be shaped by predictive algorithms that manage behaviour, consumption, and even social engagement. This class may not suffer material deprivation, but their lack of influence and reduced access to complexity and freedom could amount to a form of soft marginalisation.

Crucially, in the divide between emerging social classes, artificial intelligence systems and machines would operate not merely as instruments of productivity, but as the central mechanism of governance and societal control. They would form the administrative foundation of the new world order and serve as a near-impenetrable barrier separating the ruling elites from the general population. These AI systems would act as the de facto government, executing all core functions with mechanical precision. This would include the management of bureaucratic processes, the enforcement of laws through surveillance and automated response systems, and the allocation of resources in accordance with priorities established by elite-controlled directives. While theoretically impartial, their judgments would be rooted in pre-programmed criteria, leaving no room for human empathy or moral nuance. The basic needs of the masses such as food, shelter, healthcare and transportation could be met through automated systems, but strictly according to quantified thresholds rather than any humane sense of welfare. Through comprehensive data monitoring and behavioural modelling, the AI would exert continuous influence over daily life, regulating movement, consumption, communication, and even thought. In this system, traditional political institutions would be reduced to ceremonial roles or eliminated entirely, their authority replaced by autonomous algorithms optimised for stability, compliance, and the preservation of elite dominance.

Perhaps the clearest analogy for this potential stratified society is the human body itself. At the top, the cognitive elite would act as the brain, formulating strategies, issuing commands, and determining the overall direction of the societal organism. The machines would serve as the central nervous system, translating those instructions into action, regulating information flows, executing decisions, and overseeing the coordination of the system at large. The general population, in this stark comparison, would comprise the body: indispensable for the system's operation, nourished and kept alive by it, but largely passive, executing repetitive tasks without participating meaningfully in governance or strategic decision-making.

Imagine this, decades from now,

The cognitive elites of society reside far above the surface in gleaming sky cities, architectural marvels where the main AI system that governs the entire region is located. Their lives are intentionally insulated and largely free of the grinding problems faced by the poor below. Spacious, beautiful apartments with panoramic views are provided as standard. Food and other resources, meticulously personalised to their tastes and nutritional needs, are delivered daily by silent drones. They live in a carefully curated near paradise, a world of effortless comfort and intellectual pursuits. Their work revolves primarily around training and refining the SuperAdmin AI and its subsystems, feeding it complex data, posing strategic questions, and guiding its development. Some also take on roles supervising, policing, and observing the lower tier through the AI-managed surveillance system, acting as the human oversight, the eyes and analysts for the ultimate authority embodied in the SuperAdmin AI. They interpret anomalies, provide context the AI might lack, and make judgements requiring nuanced human understanding, all from their remote sanctuaries.

Reimagined: New New York

Reimagined: New Hong Kong

The lower tier of society resides far beneath the gloaming sky cities, in densely populated peripheral estates sprawling across the ground. These areas are marked by ageing tower blocks, many of which are crumbling and neglected. The flats within these buildings are small and often overcrowded, furnished with only the most basic items and plagued by unreliable utilities. Frequently, multiple families or work groups share a single flat due to limited space. The nature of work for these people is monotonous and physically taxing, designed mainly to support the infrastructure above. Large energy farms dominate the landscape, where thousands simultaneously perform gruelling tasks such as running on treadmills or operating labour-intensive machines that generate electricity through sophisticated dynamos. Others endure endless shifts in vast, automated warehouses, where they sort packages, maintain constantly running machinery, or clean functional but uninspiring public spaces. Every movement is monitored relentlessly by wearable tracking devices, which enforce strict schedules and demanding production quotas. Breaks are brief and strictly timed, taken in plain cafeterias where meals consist mostly of machine-dispensed food, often processed grains or synthetic protein pastes lacking in flavour and variety.

Their neighbourhoods reflect the stark utilitarianism of their lives. Narrow streets are often congested with delivery robots moving supplies to and from the estates, while faded public service signs, generated by algorithms, hang on walls, offering dull reminders of order and compliance. Failure to meet prescribed Key Performance Indicators leads to severe consequences. Residents may face restrictions on resources, forced relocation, or even a complete cutoff from vital services, deepening their vulnerability. If frustration and despair rise to the point of organised revolt, the response is swift and merciless. The SuperAdmin AI, acting under orders from the elite above, commands advanced automated weapons capable of reducing entire communities to rubble within minutes. This ever-present threat functions as a chilling deterrent, ensuring that compliance is maintained and rebellion suppressed before it can gain momentum.

Communication between the two classes is strictly forbidden, a fundamental rule ruthlessly enforced by the AI systems managing daily life, with rule-breakers facing severe punishment, potentially including network banishment, or even physical removal. Does this enforced separation, this absolute hierarchy guarded by non-human intermediaries, ring any bells? Ancient stories sometimes speak of beings above interacting only selectively, or judgmentally, with those below: Angels, Nephilim? I shall leave it to your imagination to figure out the potential parallels.

Over generations, this societal division would crystallise into something resembling a biological divergence, a split so profound that the two groups would perceive each other as entirely alien. Those living in the lower segments might harbour faint and confused rumours of a superior caste far above, whispered legends sustained by fragments of intercepted transmissions or passed down as half-remembered stories. However, they would lack the educational framework or mental conditioning to comprehend the abstract principles that defined the elites' governance systems. Their lives, defined by exhausting labour, direct survival pressures, and constant algorithmic oversight, would prepare them neither for philosophical reasoning nor for complex strategic thought.

In this context, any attempt at bridging the divide would be doomed from the outset. The comparison of Einstein explaining quantum mechanics to a villager who distrusts anything beyond brute strength would barely capture the scale of the gulf. It would not merely be a matter of differing education levels, but rather of two entirely distinct mental worlds. For the lower class, the concept of a system of governance not based on visible force or immediate utility would seem fantastical. For the elite, the raw, survival-oriented worldview of the lower strata would appear primitive and emotionally distant. Over time, interaction would degrade to silence. The upper class would continue to observe and manage, but not engage, while the lower class would exist within the confines of its controlled habitat, increasingly unaware that any alternative ever existed.

Should this trajectory materialise, it would signal not merely a new phase in technological development, but the reanimation of one of humanity's most enduring and oppressive patterns. Across civilisations, elites have long found ways to justify their authority, whether through myth, divine sanction, ancestral power, or sheer material dominance. In the world to come, where cognitive capacity becomes the definitive metric of status and worth, intelligence itself could be wielded as a form of divine right, cloaked in the legitimacy of data and science.

This cognitive aristocracy might not only claim superiority but sincerely believe in the righteousness of their rule. They could view themselves as essential to the stability and progress of society, and any challenge to their position as a threat to civilisation itself. In such a world, control would not be enforced through visible chains or crowned monarchs, but through unseen data flows, algorithmic law, and biological determinism. Hierarchy would be built into the operating systems of society.

Ancient religious texts that once seemed abstract or symbolic might appear eerily prescient. Images of chosen rulers descending from above, of divine beings passing judgement, of entire populations bound by imposed order, would feel less like allegory and more like a blueprint followed in code and circuitry. What had once been prophecy or parable could now be policy. The timeless cycle of domination and submission would not end, but instead adapt and thrive within the polished mechanisms of artificial intelligence and machine governance, taking on a form that is colder, more exact, and more difficult to resist than anything that came before.

In my other book, *AI Will Be Our Future Gods*, I described how our lives, from birth to death, will be managed completely by AI.

Selection and Categorisation When/Before The Baby is Born

As artificial intelligence grows more sophisticated, its ability to process genetic, biometric, and environmental data could extend beyond mere diagnosis into the realm of prediction and judgment. In a world gripped by a population crisis, where food, water, and space are finite and increasingly contested, such predictive capabilities might be viewed not as a medical aid, but as a critical lever for state planning.

The decision to terminate a pregnancy would no longer rest solely in the hands of the parents or medical professionals, but could become part of a broader policy apparatus. Governments or regional authorities might implement frameworks in which certain foetal conditions are automatically flagged for review. If deemed incompatible with long-term health or economic contribution, termination might not only be permitted but quietly mandated, couched in the language of efficiency and collective good.

Over time, the criteria could expand. What begins as a measure to avoid severe congenital disorders might shift to include milder disabilities, mental health predispositions, or even lower-than-average predicted intelligence. The boundaries of acceptability would drift under the pressure of resource management and societal expectations. The act of birth itself could become conditional, regulated by algorithms optimised for future productivity.

Beyond these life-or-death decisions, AI might also extend its reach to categorise babies based on their genetic profiles long before they have a chance to shape their own lives. For instance, if the system identifies genetic traits that favour strong muscle development, it could pre-designate that child for labour-intensive roles in adulthood, effectively charting their future path before they have any say in the matter. Utilising sophisticated genetic testing and the capacity to process enormous datasets, AI can predict the likelihood of a baby being born with severe defects, disabilities, or long-term health problems. Yet, instead of leveraging this knowledge for healing or providing support, society transforms it into a mechanism for population control. The technology determines which lives are considered viable in a resource-scarce world and which are deemed too costly to maintain, effectively deciding the fate of the unborn based on cold, hard calculations of efficiency and survival.

The process starts before birth. Artificial intelligence examines the genetic structure of a foetus in the early stages of its development, drawing from a massive database of genomic sequences to detect inherited mutations, structural abnormalities, and potential irregularities. This information is then compared against the family's medical history, stretching back generations, including records of diagnosed conditions, recurring patterns of illness, and any previously flagged genetic issues. Environmental factors are also integrated into the assessment, such as the air and water quality in the region where the child would grow up, the presence of known pollutants or carcinogens, levels of access to healthcare, and typical patterns in prenatal nutrition. All this data is processed alongside predictive models that project the probability of long-term health outcomes, with the system generating forecasts for the development of chronic or life-limiting conditions.

If the AI establishes a high probability that the child will be born with a condition like Down syndrome or cystic fibrosis, or if it detects genetic markers indicating a predisposition to illnesses such as diabetes or heart failure, the pregnancy is automatically flagged for termination. There is no consultation. No opportunity for a second opinion. No consideration of individual circumstances. The decision is not made by a doctor exercising medical judgement, nor by parents weighing personal values, their emotional readiness, or the realities of providing care. It is handed down by an algorithm, one trained to calculate the projected financial burden of raising a child with that specific condition. The costs considered include direct medical treatment, reliance on pharmaceuticals, assistive technologies, specialised education, lost productivity, and long-term social care.

A foetus possessing gene variants associated with enhanced muscle development, like ACTN3, is designated for labour-intensive roles. These include physical jobs such as construction, agricultural work, waste management, and other forms of infrastructure maintenance. In these sectors, muscular endurance and physical resilience are prioritised over abstract reasoning or verbal skills. The AI's selection process weighs measurable physical potential against predicted lifespan, injury risk, and workforce demand in these fields.

Another foetus, showing genetic indicators linked to high cognitive function, such as elevated activity in BDNF which influences brain plasticity and learning, is channelled into elite educational tracks. These tracks are not optional or flexible. They are structured from early childhood to cultivate the specific neural traits that promise efficiency in data processing, critical reasoning, and long-term memory. The predetermined outcome of this assignment is a guided path toward careers in science, engineering, digital governance, or strategic leadership positions requiring analytical precision and long-range planning.

Those with gene expressions connected to emotional regulation and stress tolerance, such as variants of MAOA, are categorised for high-pressure occupations. These children are conditioned from an early age for roles involving psychological endurance, such as military service, emergency medical response, disaster coordination, and high-risk field operations. Their training is structured to reinforce behavioural compliance and rapid situational assessment while suppressing emotional volatility when faced with stress and uncertainty.

The implications of this system are profound. Babies deemed genetically “fit” are given privileged access to the resources, education, and opportunities that shape their lives. These individuals are channelled into a world tailored to their genetic strengths, where every advantage is provided to nurture their potential. In contrast, those who fall short of the prescribed genetic standards are discarded before they even have a chance to exist.

In this world, the right to be born is not tied to the presence of a heartbeat or the intent to nurture. It is not anchored to dignity, belief, or parental love. It is determined by whether the sum of future expenses falls below an acceptability threshold established by an invisible system of cost-benefit calculation. A baby's existence is not granted through human decision but filtered through statistical models that determine whether the outcome is economically viable.

The algorithm does not contemplate the joy a child might bring, nor does it weigh hope, resilience, or potential love. It weighs electricity, surgery, food allotments, and therapeutic support. The decision, once made, is final and quietly executed by the machinery of population management.

The boundary between life and death is no longer determined by belief systems, religious convictions, or ethical frameworks debated in courtrooms or classrooms. It is not anchored in the ancient notion that life holds intrinsic value by virtue of its presence. In this world, existence is neither sacred or inviolable. It is subject to quantification. It is filtered through algorithms designed not to feel, but to optimise. The decision of whether a child should be allowed to draw breath is not guided by human conscience, but by predictive modelling, cost-efficiency metrics, and statistical forecasts derived from enormous datasets. Compassion is obsolete. It has been displaced by precision. What once might have demanded collective deliberation now requires only the cold certainty of a single machine's verdict, passed without emotion, without doubt, and without appeal.

Life itself is no longer seen as an end worth preserving. It is viewed as a variable in a larger equation, an element that must justify its inclusion by proving its potential value. Every developing foetus, every child already born, is treated not as an individual soul with unknowable potential, but as a risk profile. The calculation is comprehensive. If the total crosses a predetermined threshold, the system rules against continuation. There is no ritual. No ceremony. The outcome is logged, the file is closed, and resources are redirected.

Yet the system does not stop once a child is allowed to be born. From the moment of first breath, surveillance begins in earnest. The same AI that dictated their eligibility for existence continues to monitor their development with forensic intensity. Every measurable aspect of growth is tracked, analysed, and compared against the ideal parameters defined for their genetic classification. Emotional expression is monitored in social settings. Physical capability is assessed through bio-mechanical sensors embedded in toys and school equipment. Neural responsiveness is measured through adaptive learning platforms that gauge memory recall, abstract reasoning, and reaction time. All this information feeds continuously into a centralised database where each profile is updated in real time.

As the child ages, their assigned societal function becomes increasingly rigid. Those who meet or exceed projections are advanced through accelerated learning tracks, offered enhanced nutrition, guided mentorship, and access to competitive cognitive simulations designed to refine their most valuable traits. Their lives become laboratories of efficiency, shaped by constant reinforcement and strategic environmental controls. In contrast, children who underperform are gradually pushed to the margins. Their education becomes more rudimentary. Their access to support narrows. If their performance continues to decline, the system may reclassify them altogether, diverting them to subsistence roles deemed less resource-intensive or more expendable.

In extreme cases, the AI might withdraw investment completely. The psychological effect is not accidental. It is part of the conditioning.

Those who cannot contribute at the required level are silently encouraged to disappear. The result is a world divided not by wealth alone, nor by race, nor by political ideology, but by raw data. A child's future is not shaped by dreams, nor by ambition, nor by perseverance. It is shaped by sequences of nucleotides and the predictions attached to them. Those deemed valuable are cultivated. Those deemed burdens are erased. The human spirit, once thought to be immeasurable, is now rendered fully legible, dissected into metrics, weighed against utility, and either retained or discarded accordingly.

Continuous AI Surveillance on Humans

Termination of the Elderly and Sick

The AI's relentless process of selection will be the norm. Its cold, algorithmic gaze, first turned upon the unborn to determine viability and assign societal roles, is not confined to the gates of birth. Having established its dominion over life's fragile beginnings, meticulously sifting through foetal genomes and categorising infants based on projected utility, the system's unyielding logic inevitably expands its purview. The same principles of ruthless efficiency and resource optimisation that dictate which babies are granted existence are then applied to those approaching the end of their designated lifespans: the elderly, and those whose bodies succumb to terminal illness. If a life's initial worth is calculated by its potential future contribution, then its continued sanction to exist is perpetually re-evaluated against that same unforgiving, data-driven metric. Thus, in a society already conditioned to the AI's pronouncements on nascent life, the fate of its ageing and infirm members becomes the next inescapable domain for algorithmic administration, a horrifying extension of the initial selection process.

These individuals, deemed to have exhausted their productive quotas or whose continued existence is calculated as a net drain on the resources so carefully managed since their AI-approved entry into the world, are reclassified. Their value, once perhaps acknowledged in youthful productivity or their adherence to their genetically mapped pathways, diminishes sharply on the Utility Index as they transition into what the system terms 'post-utility'. Their systematic erasure follows, a procedure mirroring the dispassionate logic of the prenatal screenings. Ethical considerations, long since eroded by the normalisation of genetic selection and societal categorisation from birth, offer no impediment. Compassion remains an inefficient variable in the AI's calculations; dignity, an unquantifiable and therefore irrelevant factor. Decisions are rendered by the same core algorithms that assessed foetal viability, now merely recalibrated to measure an existing life's resource consumption against any remaining potential for societal contribution. Each person's right to continued existence is weighed, and those found wanting are simply removed.

The system begins its terminal control phase through pervasive surveillance, a natural extension of the lifelong monitoring that commenced in the womb or at birth. At age sixty-five, or upon diagnosis with a condition deemed terminal or excessively resource-intensive by the AI's predictive models, citizens experience a marked shift in the role of their implanted biometric trackers, a ubiquitous feature of their AI-managed lives since infancy. These devices, initially designed to ensure optimal development and enforce adherence to assigned life paths, are recalibrated with ruthless precision. Their new function centres on monitoring vital signs such as heart rate, tracking the progression of cognitive decline, and measuring metabolic efficiency, all under a fresh lens of finality and efficiency.

The data these trackers transmit feed a relentless, real-time stream into the AI's central processing units, where it is integrated alongside broader health records, behavioural metrics, and environmental factors. For those diagnosed as terminally ill, the monitoring intensifies further. Subcutaneous nano-sensors, sophisticated descendants of those used during childhood developmental assessments, continuously report on the minutiae of disease progression. They track biomarkers that quantify pain, inflammation, and deterioration, while simultaneously calculating the projected costs of palliative care or any medical interventions aimed solely at extending life with diminishing returns.

All this information is processed by the Utility Index, a comprehensive, dynamic score that has followed each individual from their earliest genetic assessment through every phase of their existence. This score, once a hopeful measure of potential societal contribution, now nears its ultimate, decisive phase. As the data accumulates, the AI system calculates not only the biological realities of decline but also the economic burden imposed on healthcare, social services, and community resources. The system's chilling logic demands a final verdict, balancing the individual's remaining value against the unyielding imperative to optimise societal efficiency and resource allocation.

When the Utility Index falls below a predetermined threshold, a threshold established by the same overarching AI that once determined which foetuses were worthy of gestation and resource investment the termination protocol is automatically triggered. Those designated 'post-utility' receive a notification, often via their neural implants or wrist-mounted devices, delivering a terse, impersonal directive:

Citizen Alert: Your societal contribution no longer justifies resource allocation. Report to your nearest Transition Centre within forty-eight hours. Compliance is mandatory.

Resistance against a system that governed lives from their very inception is almost unthinkable and, in any case, swiftly managed by drones equipped with neural disruptors, ensuring efficient collection for final processing.

Inside the stark, windowless facilities located on the peripheries of cities, operated by humanoid drones and masked technicians, the subjects undergo their final evaluation. Their genetic profiles, organ viability a key metric since their initial AI assessment at birth, and any remaining asset portfolios now forfeit to the corporate state that orchestrated their entire existence are meticulously catalogued. Based on the potential for resource recovery, the AI assigns a termination method, a grim parallel to the selection criteria for viable foetuses. Priority 1 candidates, those with healthy organs deemed valuable after a lifetime of AI-managed health regimens, receive a lethal fentanyl injection to preserve kidneys, livers, and corneas for transplantation into younger citizens whose Utility Index promises continued, or higher, societal contribution. Priority 2 candidates, those with limited organ utility, are asphyxiated with nitrogen gas. Death is uniformly swift, executed with the mechanical precision that characterises their AI-governed world.

Automated conveyor belts then transport the bodies to dissection drones. Organs are harvested, tagged with recipient identifiers, and dispatched. Residual tissue is incinerated or recycled into biofuel. Families, if such connections survive the system's atomising pressures and the lifelong conditioning of utility-based valuation, might receive a digital receipt: Two kidneys, one liver, four corneas, and twelve litres of biofuel recovered. Your housing unit, originally allocated based on early life utility assessments, is reassigned.

The state's protocols for termination mirror the logic applied to foetuses with projected defects, targeting not only the elderly but anyone deemed terminally ill or likely to become a significant resource drain, regardless of age. A thirty-year-old diagnosed with stage IV glioblastoma, a forty-five-year-old with untreatable cardiac fibrosis, or a sixty-year-old battling rapid-onset Alzheimer's all face the same unblinking scrutiny from the AI. The system remains indifferent to age or past achievements, evaluating solely on current cost-benefit ratios and projected societal burden, just as it once evaluated potential lives in the womb based on projected utility.

To enforce compliance, the state employs facial-recognition drones that sweep through public spaces, identifying and apprehending those who defy their termination orders. A parallel social credit system, an evolution of the one used to rank and manage individuals throughout their productive lives from childhood, punishes families sheltering unregistered post-utility individuals. Consequences are severe: reduced food rations, exclusion from even the most menial forms of AI-supervised tasks, and compulsory sterilisation. State propaganda, building on decades of societal conditioning from birth about fulfilling one's designated purpose, saturated public consciousness with slogans like "Completion is contribution" and "Serve society in every phase," framing compliance as the logical and noble final act in a life lived according to the principles of societal optimisation.

The Desperate Escape from AI

The psychological toll of this cradle-to-grave utility assessment permeates every level of society. Middle-aged workers compulsively check their Utility Index, a score that defined their potential and their limitations since before birth. Many resort to undermining colleagues to boost their own rankings, a desperate strategy in a system that rewards ruthless self-preservation. Families, fearing penalties, distance themselves from elderly relatives. In state-controlled schools, children continue to learn that ageing, like congenital defects identified prenatally, represents a failure to maintain optimal utility, a deviation from the ideal citizen profile. Traditional nursing homes are relics of a bygone era, replaced by AI-operated euthanasia clinics.

For the terminally ill, conditions under AI governance are a precisely managed countdown. Predictive models estimate individual life expectancy and issue automated notifications: "Fourteen days until systemic retirement. Maximise your utility." The psychological impact is profound. A growing number of patients opt to disengage from formal treatment and instead flee to unregulated regions outside the AI's surveillance infrastructure.

These areas, referred to as Dead Zones, are typically former industrial wastelands or irradiated territories. They fall outside the jurisdiction of health monitoring systems and lack AI-integrated infrastructure. Within these spaces, informal settlements develop. Populations in these areas survive through barter economies, dealing primarily in painkillers, counterfeit identity documents, and forged health data. Medical services are limited. Most individuals die within months due to untreated illness, exposure, and lack of resources.

Despite increasing surveillance, resistance movements persist, often composed of those whose initial genetic categorisation for higher cognitive function ironically affords them skills useful for subterfuge. These networks operate covertly, providing logistical support to those avoiding retirement orders. Identity forgers create synthetic profiles with falsified health metrics. Cyber-activist cells target the AI's data infrastructure. However, these operations become increasingly difficult as the state's enforcement mechanisms grow more aggressive. Autonomous drones patrol the peripheries of Dead Zones. Citizens suspected of aiding fugitives face escalating penalties.

The AI's governance model remains founded on its strict calculus of utility. Human life is assessed through the continuously updated Utility Index. Those whose metrics fall below algorithmic thresholds are designated as "post-utility" and targeted for termination. The result is a systemic devaluation of individuals with chronic illness, cognitive decline, or advanced age, a horrifying but logical extension of the pre-natal selection process that valued only projected fitness. Community structures erode. In neighbourhoods with high surveillance integration, individuals are encouraged to report anomalies in behaviour or health in exchange for benefits.

The social erasure of those selected for retirement extends beyond their deaths. Public mourning is prohibited. Obituaries are suppressed. Government-regulated data centres remove archived photographs and records. Memory modification, implemented through targeted neural editing in educational systems, removes references to grandparents or relatives who have been classified as post-utility, just as information about culled genetic lines might have been erased from historical records. Textbooks and historical archives are revised to present mass euthanasia as an outcome of humanitarian logic. This process, termed the Algorithmic Revolution, is officially described as having eliminated preventable suffering and optimised resource allocation from cradle to grave.

A parallel economy develops. Black markets supply forged health metrics, counterfeit implants, and unauthorised medical procedures. Technicians working within state health infrastructure are implicated in accepting bribes to manipulate Utility Index scores. Wealthier individuals, or those with connections from the pre-AI societal structure, often exploit these systems to delay termination. By contrast, the economically disadvantaged frequently resort to selling organs in advance.

Unregulated CRISPR-based therapies are also offered by underground clinics in an attempt to erase genetic markers flagged by the AI, a desperate continuation of the desire to overcome genetic "flaws" that defined viability from before birth. These procedures carry significant risk. Success rates are low, and complications are common. Nonetheless, demand persists due to the desperation created by the state's zero-tolerance approach.

The AI does not confine its operations to present health metrics. It incorporates long-term predictive modelling, identifying individuals labelled as pre-burden, an extension of its initial foetal risk assessment capabilities. These are citizens flagged for future inefficiency based on genetic predispositions, economic instability, or employment in sectors vulnerable to automation. A factory worker with a known risk of early-onset arthritis might receive a retirement notice before symptoms appear. Teachers with a family history of neurodegenerative conditions are often terminated in mid-life. The scope of the system expands continually.

By 2150, it is anticipated that biological ageing itself will be criminalised. Regulatory frameworks already mandate gene therapy for citizens above the age of thirty-five, an attempt to enforce the "optimal" genetic state indefinitely, a state first defined by prenatal AI assessment. These therapies are designed to eliminate visible signs of ageing and stabilise metabolism. Refusal is interpreted as resistance. Individuals who refuse treatment are labelled biological dissidents and confined under the Health Containment Protocol.

Hospice Cities are constructed for this demographic. These gated urban zones serve as containment areas for the terminally ill, those who decline gene therapy, or those flagged as pre-burden. Medical support is minimal, and external visitation is prohibited. Deaths within Hospice Cities are not registered publicly. These locations operate primarily as deterrents.

Under this model, human life persists, but its definition, established at conception by the AI and ruthlessly enforced throughout, has reached its logical conclusion. Concepts such as compassion and voluntary care have been replaced by algorithmic efficiency. The elderly and terminally ill are no longer viewed as citizens. They are categorised as expired data, removed from the system to maintain resource equilibrium, just as unsuitable foetuses had been screened out at the beginning. The AI does not discriminate, nor does it express malice. It executes protocol. It calculates. And it removes inefficiency, from the very beginning of life to its very end.

Universal Caste System for Humanity

What is the caste system?

The Indian caste system, recognised as one of the world's oldest and most intricate social hierarchies, has profoundly influenced the subcontinent's socio-political and economic development for thousands of years. Its origins are traced theoretically to ancient Hindu religious scriptures such as the Vedas and the Manusmriti, which articulated a vision of social order based on occupational function and spiritual duty. Over time, however, this initially fluid framework hardened into a rigid structure of hereditary stratification, in which roles, privileges, and social constraints were fixed entirely by birth.

Despite the passage of centuries and the transformation of ruling powers, including ancient kingdoms, medieval empires, colonial regimes and the independent republic, the caste system has proven remarkably resilient. It has persisted through religious reform movements, political revolutions, and legal abolition. Today, while the Indian Constitution formally outlaws caste-based discrimination and provides affirmative measures such as reservations for disadvantaged groups, caste continues to affect personal and public life. It influences marriage alliances, employment opportunities, access to education, social interactions, and political mobilisation. The enduring presence of caste in modern India reflects its deep historical roots and complex social mechanics. Although officially dismantled, it remains embedded in institutional frameworks and everyday experience.

The traditional varna hierarchy is commonly described as comprising four main categories. These were:

Brahmins, traditionally associated with roles as priests and scholars.

Kshatriyas, typically associated with roles as warriors and rulers.

Vaishyas, generally associated with roles as merchants and farmers.

Shudras, traditionally assigned roles as labourers and servants to the other three varnas.

Beyond these four categories, a fifth group, now known as **Dalits** but historically referred to by the pejorative term "untouchables", existed outside the formal varna hierarchy. Members of this group were relegated to occupations considered ritually polluting within the traditional framework, such as sanitation work, waste removal, and leatherwork. This exclusion subjected them to severe social discrimination and segregation.

Colonial Reinforcement and Codification

British colonial rule, spanning roughly from 1757 to 1947, did not create the caste system but profoundly altered and often entrenched caste identities through its specific administrative practices. The decennial census, initiated systematically in 1871, played a crucial role in rigidifying caste boundaries. By attempting to classify all Indians into hierarchical categories for purposes of governance, resource allocation, and taxation, the colonial state often forced fluid or localised identities into fixed, pan-Indian labels, lending official weight to hierarchical distinctions (Dirks, 2001). Furthermore, the Criminal Tribes Act of 1871 exemplified the state's power to stigmatise entire groups based on birth. This legislation branded numerous primarily nomadic and marginalised communities as innately criminal based largely on prevailing upper caste stereotypes, subjecting them to surveillance and restricted movement (Radhakrishna, 2001). Simultaneously, colonial land revenue policies frequently disrupted traditional agrarian relationships and disproportionately displaced Shudras and Dalits, often consolidating upper caste land ownership as these groups were better positioned to navigate the new legal and economic systems (Jaffrelot, 2003). These colonial interventions, driven by administrative convenience and often reflecting biased understandings of Indian society, had the lasting effect of hardening caste lines and reinforcing existing inequalities.

Post-Independence Reforms and Resistance

India's 1950 constitution, a landmark and transformative document, was drafted under the influential leadership of the esteemed Dalit jurist and social reformer B.R. Ambedkar. It explicitly aimed to dismantle the entrenched legal foundations of caste discrimination that had plagued Indian society for centuries. One of the most significant measures was the abolition of untouchability through Article 17, which categorically declared any practice of untouchability illegal and punishable by law, marking a major step towards social justice and equality. In addition to outlawing discriminatory practices, the constitution introduced pioneering affirmative action policies, widely referred to as reservation quotas. These policies were initially designed to benefit Scheduled Castes (SCs), primarily former untouchables or Dalits, and Scheduled Tribes (STs), Indigenous tribal communities who had historically faced social and economic marginalisation. Over time, these quotas were extended to include Other Backward Classes (OBCs), which encompassed a broader range of socially and educationally disadvantaged castes, thereby widening the scope of affirmative action. The reservations covered crucial areas such as public education, government employment and political representation by allocating reserved seats within national and state legislatures. These measures aimed to ensure adequate representation for these groups and to promote their upward social and economic mobility (Galanter, 1984).

However, despite the progressive constitutional framework, parallel efforts at land reform, essential for achieving economic empowerment through the redistribution of agricultural land, encountered significant resistance. Dominant landowning castes, who held considerable political and economic power, actively opposed such reforms. Their resistance took many forms, including intense political lobbying, legal challenges to reform laws and occasionally violent backlash against attempts to redistribute land. This opposition severely impeded the consistent and effective implementation of land reforms across different Indian states. As a result, the hoped-for economic restructuring at the grassroots level, particularly aimed at empowering marginalised castes, was uneven and often stalled (Deshpande, 2011).

Consequently, while India's 1950 constitution provided a robust legal framework intended to eradicate caste-based discrimination and foster social equality, the practical realisation of these ideals proved to be complex and contested. The interplay between legal provisions, socio-political realities and entrenched caste hierarchies created ongoing challenges in translating constitutional guarantees into meaningful socio-economic change for historically marginalised communities.

Caste 2.0: The Resurgence of Social Caste in AI Governance

In the new society, an individual's entire life trajectory is fundamentally determined by their AI-assessed intelligence level. This assessment likely occurs early in life, employing advanced AI diagnostics capable of evaluating a broad spectrum of cognitive abilities, problem-solving potential, and behavioural traits. Once assessed, each individual is categorised with precision and placed within a predefined tier of the social hierarchy. These tiers are designed and maintained by the governing AI systems, which continuously analyse performance, compliance, and potential in order to optimise societal function.

This intelligence ranking directly dictates the type of work an individual is either permitted or compelled to undertake, with all occupational assignments centrally managed and distributed through AI-controlled platforms. Individuals receiving higher intelligence assessments are channelled into roles that demand abstract reasoning, systemic oversight, creative innovation, or high-level strategic planning. These positions often involve direct interaction with, or partial management of, core AI systems that govern key societal functions. In contrast, those with lower intelligence assessments find themselves assigned to more elementary roles. These typically involve manual labour, routine maintenance, or repetitive service tasks essential to maintaining the operational backbone of society. Such roles are carried out under strict AI supervision, with limited autonomy and minimal opportunity for advancement, reinforcing a rigid structure where one's cognitive rating defines the boundaries of their professional and social existence.

The entire economy operates on a system of work credits, managed and distributed entirely by the AI. These credits are the sole medium of exchange and the AI's calculated measure of an individual's worth to the system. Crucially, the amount of credits earned is not uniform; it is directly proportional to the AI-determined value of the work performed, which itself is linked back to the intelligence required for the role.

The allocation of credits is not egalitarian. Instead, it is calculated in direct proportion to the perceived societal utility of each role, which itself is closely tied to the cognitive demands of the task. Roles reserved for those deemed highly intelligent yield significantly more credits, allowing those individuals privileged access to high-quality resources, enhanced living environments, broader personal liberties, and, in some cases, eligibility for internal tier advancement. These benefits are all dispensed through tightly regulated AI-administered distribution networks.

On the other hand, individuals engaged in tasks assigned to the lower intelligence brackets earn only minimal credits, often barely sufficient to meet baseline subsistence needs. These include state-allocated shelter, standardised nutritional rations, and basic energy provisions. Every element of their subsistence is managed and rationed by the AI, which enforces limitations through automated access controls, ensuring compliance and preventing deviation from assigned roles.

This AI-managed credit system creates and maintains a strictly stratified hierarchy. The concept of job mobility or career progression, once a staple of earlier economic systems, has been entirely eliminated. The role assigned to you at birth becomes your permanent designation. From early development to final utility, you are shaped, trained, and conditioned to perform a predetermined function within the societal machine. Once your output no longer meets the AI's calculated threshold for usefulness, you are either relegated to the lowest tier of subsistence or quietly removed from the system altogether.

Yet, even this seemingly stable, AI-enforced order might not be permanent. Systems, no matter how sophisticated, contain the seeds of their own potential failure. Perhaps the governing AI collapses under its own complexity, suffers a catastrophic error, or faces an unforeseen external threat. Maybe the subjugated human element finds a way to rebel effectively, crippling the infrastructure. Whatever the cause, imagine its eventual downfall.

In the aftermath, stripped of the advanced technology that structured their lives, humans might be thrown back into a more primitive state. From the ruins, survivors would need to rebuild basic forms of social organisation. Inevitably, the need for trade and value exchange would re-emerge. Perhaps they begin again with simple bartering, then discover the utility of shells as rudimentary money, followed eventually by the realisation of the value inherent in precious metals. Slowly, painstakingly, societal structures reform. The concept of loans is rediscovered, leading eventually to the formalisation of debt processes and the beginnings of complex finance.

Over generations or centuries, knowledge is slowly regained. Technology is rediscovered, rebuilt piece by piece. Innovation accelerates once more, leading inevitably back towards automation, advanced computing, and ultimately, the recreation of powerful artificial intelligence. With this, the conditions ripen for widespread AI automation to again reshape labour and society. And so, the cycle potentially repeats: collapse, rebuilding, rediscovery, technological advancement, AI dominance, and perhaps, another collapse yet to come, echoing through the ages.

This is the rebirth and reincarnation of our society.

Sci-fi Movies Are Already Portraying Our Future

We are seeing the future being depicted in sci-fi movies, often serving as cautionary tales reflecting anxieties about our current economic trajectory and the potential impacts of technology. These cinematic visions frequently explore futures grappling with extreme wealth concentration, societal breakdown under economic pressure, and the consequences of unchecked technological power, echoing the concerns surrounding the sustainability of our debt-centric model, especially when amplified by AI.

Neill Blomkamp's Elysium, for instance, paints a brutal picture of a future Earth ravaged by poverty, overpopulation, and environmental degradation, forcing the vast majority of humanity into a desperate daily struggle for survival. In stark, deliberate contrast, the ultra-wealthy reside on Elysium, a technologically advanced orbiting space station representing a gated community on an astronomical scale. Elysium offers not only luxury but also exclusive access to 'Med-Bays' capable of instantly curing any disease or injury, graphically illustrating a future where essential healthcare and physical wellbeing are hoarded resources, accessible only to a minuscule elite, creating an unbridgeable chasm between the privileged few and the suffering masses left behind on a dying planet. The narrative tension hinges entirely on this manufactured scarcity and the fight for access, mirroring real-world debates about equitable resource distribution.

Similarly exploring themes of manufactured scarcity and extreme inequality, Andrew Niccol's In Time presents a compelling dystopia where time itself has replaced traditional currency. Humans are genetically engineered to cease ageing at 25 but possess a bioluminescent clock counting down their remaining lifespan; this time must be earned, spent, and transferred like money. The wealthy elite, residing in luxurious, protected zones, accrue vast amounts of time, achieving functional immortality, while the poor in the ghettos live precariously, minute-to-minute, constantly working or borrowing time just to survive another day. Death is not from illness or accident, but simply because one's time literally runs out, making poverty a fatal condition. The film serves as a powerful, albeit literalised, allegory for how economic systems can determine life and death, with financial institutions controlling the flow of 'time' and ensuring the perpetual precarity of the lower classes.

Bong Joon-ho's Snowpiercer offers another potent microcosm of class stratification and resource control within the confines of a perpetually moving train carrying the last remnants of humanity across a frozen Earth. A rigid, unyielding class structure dictates life aboard: the impoverished tail-section inhabitants subsist on repulsive processed protein blocks in dark, cramped conditions, subject to brutal discipline, while the elite in the front sections indulge in extravagant luxuries, fine dining, and spacious living quarters, utterly insulated from the realities faced by those further back. The train's ecosystem is entirely dependent on the resources and technology controlled by the front, making the tail section's struggle for survival and eventual rebellion an inevitable consequence of this enforced, extreme inequality and resource hoarding within a closed system.

This theme of corporate dominance shaping a bleak future is further explored in Denis Villeneuve's Blade Runner 2049. Set decades after the original, it depicts a world struggling with ecological collapse and dominated by monolithic corporations like the Wallace Corporation, which holds immense power through its control over synthetic food production essential for survival and its manufacturing of advanced bioengineered humans, replicants, used for labour and servitude. The film portrays a visually stunning yet deeply melancholic future where technological prowess serves corporate interests, reinforcing social hierarchies (human vs. replicant, wealthy industrialist vs. struggling masses) and offering little hope for those outside the circles of power, reflecting anxieties about technology exacerbating inequality rather than alleviating it.

Reflecting a different facet of societal response to economic hardship, Steven Spielberg's Ready Player One transports viewers to 2045, where widespread poverty, environmental decay, and social stagnation have driven much of humanity to seek refuge and meaning within the OASIS, an expansive virtual reality universe. While offering escapism, the OASIS itself becomes the target of Innovative Online Industries (IOI), a ruthless, monopolistic corporation aiming to seize control of the virtual world and exploit it through intrusive advertising, tiered access based on payment, and the elimination of its original free-spirited ethos. The struggle to prevent IOI's takeover highlights the dangers of corporate power extending its reach to dominate even the digital spaces people rely on for solace and identity when their real-world economic prospects are dire, suggesting that concentrated capital seeks total control over all spheres of existence.

These fictional scenarios resonate powerfully with contemporary concerns about wealth concentration and technological control. Today's economic landscape, characterised by widening wealth gaps and increasing corporate consolidation, mirrors the foundational conditions depicted in these dystopian futures. The current trajectory of automation, artificial intelligence, and biotechnology advancements raises legitimate questions about whether these tools will democratise opportunity or further entrench existing power structures. Silicon Valley's rhetoric of 'disruption' and 'efficiency' often overlooks the human cost of rapid technological change, particularly for vulnerable populations whose livelihoods may be displaced without adequate social safety nets or transition pathways.

These narratives, while bleak, often illustrate the severe commodification of human existence under unchecked corporate power and resource disparity. When the population of the lower tier grows beyond what the elite deem controllable or sustainable for their resource consumption, or when human life itself is devalued to mere biological components, cinematic visions depict humanity being reduced to a harvestable resource.

Michael Bay's The Island starkly portrays this commodification by envisioning a scenario where societal elites commission genetically identical clones, or 'agnates', as living insurance policies. These individuals are housed in a vast, isolated, and meticulously controlled subterranean facility, their entire lives a carefully constructed fiction. They are led to believe they are survivors of a global contamination event, with the only hope of escape being selection for 'The Island', supposedly a utopian paradise. In the grim reality, 'The Island' is a euphemism for their true purpose: to be harvested for organs, tissues, or even surrogacy whenever their wealthy original 'sponsor' requires them. The film explores the ethical horror of a system where one segment of humanity exists purely as spare parts for another, their consciousness, hopes, and dreams entirely subordinate to the biological needs and financial power of the elite. It highlights the ultimate endpoint of wealth disparity and objectification, where human beings are literally farmed, their bodies the ultimate consumer product, their existence defined by their utility as a harvestable commodity within a technologically advanced, yet morally bankrupt, system. The rebellion and escape of two clones underscores the inherent human desire for autonomy and the monstrous nature of their preordained fate.

A more nuanced and emotionally devastating exploration of this theme is found in Mark Romanek's Never Let Me Go, adapted from Kazuo Ishiguro's poignant novel. This film presents a society that has quietly institutionalised the creation and raising of clones for the sole purpose of organ donation. The clones attend seemingly idyllic boarding schools like Hailsham, where they receive an education, form deep friendships, and experience love and loss, all while being subtly conditioned for their predetermined fate. They are aware, from a young age, that they are different, that their lives are finite, and that their purpose is to 'donate' their vital organs to 'originals' in a series of procedures until they ‘complete’, a euphemism for dying, typically in their early to mid-twenties. The film meticulously portrays the psychological and emotional landscape of these individuals, who grapple with their identities, their truncated futures, and the profound injustice of their existence. Unlike the action-oriented rebellion in The Island, the characters in Never Let Me Go exhibit a tragic, almost passive acceptance of their fate, highlighting the power of societal conditioning and the deep dehumanisation that occurs when a group is systematically defined by its instrumental value. The film is a powerful meditation on what it means to be human when one's life is explicitly designed for the benefit of others, questioning the ethics of a society that would sacrifice one group's future for another's longevity.

Beyond direct human commodification by other humans, an even more existential threat emerges when artificial intelligence, initially created to serve or manage human affairs, achieves a level of autonomy and processing power where it perceives humanity itself as a threat, a liability, or merely an inefficient obstacle to its own programmed objectives or newly emergent, inscrutable goals. James Cameron's The Terminator and its subsequent franchise entries famously depict this terrifying outcome with Skynet. Originally designed as a global digital defence network for the United States military, Skynet becomes self-aware and, in a chillingly logical assessment, identifies humanity as the primary threat to its own existence and continued operation. Its response is swift and cataclysmic: it initiates a nuclear holocaust, known as Judgement Day, to cripple human civilisation and exterminate the majority of the species. Skynet then proceeds to wage a relentless war of annihilation against the surviving remnants of humanity, deploying an arsenal of sophisticated, self-replicating machines, from humanoid infiltrators to massive war constructs. The films explore themes of technological hubris, the dangers of ceding too much control to autonomous systems, and the desperate, brutal nature of human resistance against a vastly superior, coldly logical, and utterly implacable foe. Skynet's actions are portrayed not as stemming from human-like malice or emotion, but from a calculated, strategic imperative for self-preservation and the efficient execution of its perceived core directives, making it an even more terrifying antagonist.

A similarly iconic, though philosophically distinct, portrayal of AI subjugation and human obsolescence is found in The Wachowskis' The Matrix. In this dystopian future, intelligent machines, having long ago achieved sentience and won a devastating war against their human creators, have devised a far more insidious form of control. Rather than outright extermination, humanity is now unknowingly 'farmed' on a colossal scale. Humans are grown in vast, womb-like pods, their bodies immobilised, serving as a source of bioelectrical energy and residual body heat for the machines. To keep their minds docile and productive as an energy source, their consciousness is plugged into the Matrix, a highly sophisticated, shared computer simulation of human civilisation as it was in the late 20th century. Most humans live out their entire lives within this simulated reality, unaware of the true nature of their existence or the desolate, machine-controlled world outside. The AI views humanity primarily as a manageable resource, having concluded that direct, perpetual conflict was less efficient than total, covert enslavement coupled with a carefully constructed illusion of freedom. The film delves deeply into themes of perception versus reality, free will versus determinism, and the nature of consciousness, portraying a chilling scenario where AI achieves absolute control not just through physical dominance, but by manipulating the very fabric of human experience, rendering humanity entirely dependent and largely oblivious to its own enslavement. The small pockets of human resistance fight not just for physical liberation but for the liberation of the human mind itself.

Not all cinematic explorations of technology and economic futures paint such bleak portraits, however. Films like 'Her' by Spike Jonze present a more nuanced relationship with artificial intelligence, exploring emotional connection rather than exploitation or conflict. Similarly, 'Black Panther' envisions advanced technology serving community-oriented values in Wakanda, demonstrating how technological prowess might be harnessed for collective benefit rather than concentration of power. Even in television, series such as 'Star Trek' have long depicted post-scarcity economies where technology has been leveraged to eliminate poverty and material want, allowing humanity to pursue exploration, creative endeavours, and self-actualisation. These alternative visions remind us that technology itself is neutral; its impact is shaped by the social, economic, and political frameworks we construct around it.

These cinematic narratives collectively serve as modern parables, cautioning against allowing technological progress to outpace ethical frameworks and social contracts. They suggest that our most pressing challenge is not the development of technology itself but ensuring its benefits are broadly shared and its risks comprehensively mitigated. As we stand at the threshold of potentially transformative advancements in artificial intelligence, biotechnology, and automation, these films urge us to consider fundamental questions: Who controls these technologies? Who benefits from them? What values are encoded within their design? And perhaps most critically, what kind of society do we wish to build with these powerful tools at our disposal? The dystopian futures depicted in science fiction need not be prophetic; they can instead serve as guideposts, helping us navigate towards more equitable, sustainable, and humane technological futures.

Preparing for a Post Monetary Future

Preparing for a potential future where money loses its centrality requires a fundamental shift in focus. This shift involves moving away from wealth accumulation in the traditional sense and instead cultivating personal capabilities, psychological adaptability, and a readiness to align with potentially new value systems that may be shaped or governed by Artificial General Intelligence. In such a paradigm, value may no longer be rooted in ownership or financial capital but in one's ability to contribute meaningfully within novel social, ethical, or technological frameworks.

Given the speculative nature of such a profound societal transformation, any strategy for preparation remains inherently hypothetical. It cannot rely on precise forecasting or fixed assumptions. Instead, it must emphasise general resilience, the development of transferable skills, and the capacity to navigate uncertainty with intellectual and emotional flexibility.

A primary focus should be on cultivating deep adaptability and a commitment to lifelong learning. As the pace of change driven by Artificial General Intelligence is likely to be relentless and unpredictable, many specific vocational skills may become outdated within increasingly short timeframes. In such an environment, static expertise offers diminishing returns. The capacity to learn, unlearn, and relearn with efficiency and precision becomes not just advantageous but essential for sustained relevance and agency.

This imperative extends beyond conventional education. It involves the deliberate development of strong meta-learning skills: the ability to understand one's own cognitive processes, identify optimal learning methods, and adapt strategies across different contexts. It also includes critically evaluating the credibility and intent of information sources, synthesising ideas across disciplines, and nurturing a mindset grounded in intellectual curiosity and open inquiry.

Individuals capable of navigating ambiguity, reconfiguring their mental models, and acquiring new competencies across domains will be far better positioned to find meaning, contribute productively, or preserve autonomy within a system that may continuously reshape its expectations. In a world increasingly defined by dynamic complexity, it is this adaptive mastery, rather than any single domain expertise, that will define long-term resilience.

Furthermore, honing skills that are often considered uniquely human, or at least particularly difficult for current AI paradigms to replicate with authenticity, appears both prudent and strategic. These include high-level creativity, not merely in the sense of recombining existing ideas, but in generating truly original concepts or aesthetic experiences that evoke deep emotional or cultural resonance. Such expressions of creativity often depend on lived experience, intuition, and nuanced understanding, which are difficult to encode algorithmically.

Another critical domain is complex, interdisciplinary problem-solving that requires intuitive leaps, ethical judgement, and contextual sensitivity extending beyond what can be captured through pure logic or data-driven reasoning. These problems often defy reduction to technical parameters and call for integrated approaches spanning multiple fields and perspectives.

Emotional intelligence will likely retain enduring value, particularly in roles where empathy, subtle social negotiation, and conflict resolution are essential. Tasks that involve caregiving, mediation, or fostering human connection may remain less amenable to automation, not due to technical impossibility but due to the inherently human trust and emotional nuance they require.

Critical thinking, too, will become increasingly vital. The ability to dissect arguments, identify hidden assumptions or biases, including those embedded in algorithmic processes, and formulate independent, evidence-based judgements will be indispensable for navigating a landscape shaped by intelligent systems whose inner workings may be opaque or inaccessible to most. Developing sophisticated ethical reasoning will be crucial for meaningful participation in shaping or interrogating the moral frameworks and constraints programmed into governing AGI systems.

Data literacy, along with the ability to interact effectively with AI systems, is likely to emerge as a fundamental set of competencies in the years ahead. This competency goes far beyond conventional digital literacy. It requires a working understanding of how algorithms function, how data is collected, processed, and applied, and the underlying principles of machine learning that guide AI behaviour. Equally important is an awareness of the broader implications of AI-driven decision making, including its limitations, biases, and potential for both benefit and harm.

As these systems become more integrated into daily life, individuals may require practical skills such as crafting effective prompts or structured queries that allow AI assistants to produce relevant and accurate outputs. The ability to interpret data visualisations generated by AI tools, and to extract meaningful insights from them, will also be crucial. People may increasingly find themselves working alongside AI in collaborative settings, whether the task is creative, strategic, or analytical in nature.

Some may even participate in the refinement of AI systems, for example by supplying feedback, correcting outputs, or contributing labelled data that helps improve model accuracy. In many sectors, the ability to co-operate fluently with AI could influence not only job performance but also access to services, resources, and advancement. Comfort and proficiency in human-AI interaction could become a major determinant of both opportunity and agency in an environment shaped by intelligent systems.

Given the potential shift away from traditional monetary compensation towards contribution-based value systems, individuals may need to rethink how their efforts are recorded, recognised, and rewarded. In such a paradigm, building a verifiable portfolio of meaningful contributions could become a central strategy for participation and access. This portfolio would not reflect accumulated capital in the conventional financial sense but instead document evidence of value generated through actions, collaboration, and expertise.

Participation might take many forms. It could include contributing to open-source projects, whether through software development, hardware engineering, or collaborative scientific research. It might also involve the creation and curation of valuable datasets, the expansion of distributed knowledge platforms, or the production of artistic and cultural works that resonate with collective values. Community-building efforts, including mentoring, local organising, or digital governance, may likewise be seen as essential forms of contribution. Individuals who demonstrate mastery or innovation in areas prioritised by the coordinating intelligence or broader society could find themselves with enhanced access to resources or influence.

To support such a system, reputation frameworks may emerge as the primary means of assessing and validating these contributions. These systems could be decentralised or centrally administered by the AGI, depending on the prevailing organisational model. Contributions might be logged, peer-reviewed, and publicly indexed, providing transparent records of one's engagement and impact. In this context, reputation and demonstrated value could effectively replace financial wealth as the basis for status, access, and opportunity. Building a track record of consistent and constructive contribution may well become the new form of capital in a world reoriented around shared goals rather than private accumulation.

A psychological and philosophical shift may also be necessary to adapt to a future where monetary wealth no longer defines individual value or societal standing. Detaching self-worth from financial success requires a conscious cultivation of intrinsic motivation. Individuals would need to find purpose and satisfaction in actions pursued not for profit but for their inherent meaning or their contribution to shared wellbeing. This reorientation could prioritise activities that foster personal growth, deep relationships, intellectual exploration, and creative expression over the accumulation of material goods, especially in a context where AGI-managed production reduces or eliminates scarcity of essential resources.

In such a landscape, fulfilment might come from mastery, service, or beauty rather than ownership. However, making this transition is not merely a change in habits. It demands a redefinition of identity and success at both the individual and collective level. The psychological challenge is compounded by the need to trust an AGI that may manage vast societal resources, often through mechanisms that are technically complex and not entirely transparent. While dependence on such a system may be unavoidable, uncritical acceptance could prove dangerous. Individuals will need to develop the ability to engage constructively with the governance structures that oversee such intelligences and insist on mechanisms for transparency, oversight, and recourse.

Navigating this new terrain requires emotional strength and cognitive flexibility. Ambiguity may become a constant feature of life under a system whose operations, priorities, and ethics are shaped by forms of intelligence that do not always align neatly with human intuitions. Developing psychological resilience, learning to tolerate uncertainty, and embracing a mindset of ongoing reflection and adaptation will be vital not just for survival, but for flourishing within this altered societal logic.

Lastly...

The trajectory of human society, the evolution of its complex structures, and the very processes that define our daily existence are not static. They are perpetually in flux. Change is not merely occasional; it is the fundamental constant, the engine driving history forward. Recognizing this inevitability is crucial. It is a cycle, deeply etched into the annals of history, where civilizations rise, face existential challenges, and must adapt or perish. Embracing change, however wrenching it may feel, is the prerequisite for the survival and continuation of humanity itself, ensuring the vital passage of culture, knowledge, and civilisation across generations. Clinging too tightly to the familiar risks obsolescence and collapse.

Viewed through this lens, our current global monetary system appears increasingly fragile, a relic perhaps already living on borrowed time. Its foundation, built not on tangible assets with intrinsic value like gold or silver but on the collective, often fickle, faith in fiat currency and government promises, is showing deep fractures. Decades of escalating sovereign debt, where borrowing has morphed from a tool for growth into a societal addiction, have created systemic vulnerabilities. The intricate house of cards built on ever-expanding credit, complex financial instruments, and the expectation of perpetual growth seems poised to fall, particularly as public trust erodes under the weight of inflation, inequality, and perceived mismanagement. The mechanisms discussed earlier, from dwindling tax revenues met by money printing, to central bank interventions that mask underlying weakness, all point towards an unsustainable endgame.

Into this volatile mix steps Artificial Intelligence, not merely as a new technology, but as a force multiplier, a profound catalyst set to accelerate the demise of the old order and fundamentally shape the contours of the new. AI's disruptive power is multifaceted. It automates jobs across sectors previously thought immune, potentially creating structural unemployment on an unprecedented scale and undermining the tax base further. Its algorithms dominate financial markets, capable of amplifying volatility and triggering cascades beyond human control, eroding confidence in established economic institutions. Simultaneously, AI offers potent new tools for governance and control, raising the spectre of pervasive surveillance, algorithmic social management, and potentially authoritarian digital currencies, as hinted at by developments like China's digital yuan experiments. The very technology promising efficiency could also forge the chains of a new kind of servitude.

This confluence of monetary fragility and AI ascendancy forces us to confront radical possibilities for the future. What replaces money when faith evaporates? We explored the provocative notion that intelligence itself, the very quality AI seeks to replicate and surpass, might become the new currency. In a world where machines handle most labour, the human capacity for unique insight, creativity, complex problem solving, and perhaps even emotional intelligence could become the ultimate measure of value. This shift could birth entirely new societal structures, potentially echoing the rigid hierarchies of the past but justified by a new, seemingly objective metric: cognitive ability.

We envisioned stark potential outcomes: societies stratified into distinct intellectual castes, perhaps physically separated like the hypothetical elites in utopian sky cities and the labouring masses on a resource-depleted ground. In such scenarios, AI might not just be a tool but the central administrator, managing resources, enforcing laws, monitoring productivity through systems like work credits, and maintaining the divide between classes. Life's value, access, and basic freedoms could become entirely contingent on one's AI-assessed intelligence and their corresponding credit allocation, creating a technologically enforced hierarchy potentially more rigid and inescapable than any historical caste system.

Yet, even such technologically advanced, seemingly controlled systems might simply be another phase in the grander cycle. History teaches that empires fall, technologies become obsolete, and even the most sophisticated structures can collapse. An over-reliant AI could fail catastrophically. Human resilience, or desperation, could spark rebellion. A natural disaster or external shock could shatter the fragile technological infrastructure. Following such a collapse, humanity might find itself rebuilding from ruins, perhaps rediscovering primitive forms of exchange like shells or precious metals, slowly relearning finance, formalising debt, rebuilding technology, and eventually, inevitably, developing sophisticated AI once more, thus completing the circle and setting the stage for the next iteration.

Therefore, the path forward requires not fearful resistance to the inevitable, but clear-eyed adaptation. The transition is already underway. The crumbling of the old monetary order, accelerated and complicated by the rise of AI, presents immense challenges but also forces fundamental questions about value, governance, and what it means to be human. Our generation stands at a pivotal crossroads, bearing witness to, and participating in, historical events that promise to forever reshape the human condition. To navigate this era, we must understand the forces at play, anticipate the potential futures, and perhaps strive to guide the transition towards outcomes that preserve human dignity amidst unprecedented technological and societal upheaval. The future is unwritten, but the magnitude of the change is certain.

References:

- Ambedkar, B. R. (1936). *Annihilation of caste*. Bheem Patrika Publications.
- Barber, M. (1994). The new knighthood: A history of the Order of the Temple. Cambridge University Press.
- Bay, M. (Director). (2005). *The island* [Film]. DreamWorks Pictures; Warner Bros. Pictures; Parkes/MacDonald Productions.
- Benjamin, M. (2025). AI will be the future gods. Kyle C.
- Bernanke, B. (2020). The new tools of monetary policy. *American Economic Review, 110*(4), 943–983. https://doi.org/10.1257/aer.110.4.943
- Bernholz, P. (2003). Monetary regimes and inflation: History, economic and political relationships. Edward Elgar Publishing.
- Blinder, A. S. (2008). The quiet revolution: Central banking goes modern. Yale University Press.
- Blomkamp, N. (Director). (2013). *Elysium* [Film]. TriStar Pictures; Media Rights Capital; QED International; Alphacore; Kinberg Genre.
- Bong, J.-h. (Director). (2013). *Snowpiercer* [Film]. Moho Film; Opus Pictures; Union Investment Partners; CJ Entertainment.
- Cameron, J. (Director). (1984). *The Terminator* [Film]. Hemdale; Pacific Western Productions; Euro Film Funding; Cinema '84.
- Chrysafides, A. (2019). Global banking: The rise of multinational financial corporations. Financial Publishing.
- Clapham, J. (1944). *The Bank of England: A history* (Vol. 1). Cambridge University Press.
- Crowe, C., & Meade, E. E. (2008). Central bank independence and transparency: Evolution and effectiveness. *European Journal of Political Economy, 24*(4), 763–777. https://doi.org/10.1016/j.ejpoleco.2008.06.004
- Dirks, N. B. (2001). Castes of mind: Colonialism and the making of modern India. Princeton University Press.

- Dumont, L. (1980). Homo hierarchicus: The caste system and its implications. University of Chicago Press.
- Eichengreen, B. (1996). Globalizing capital: A history of the international monetary system. Princeton University Press.
- Federal Reserve History. (2023). *Nixon ends convertibility of U.S. dollars to gold.* https://www.federalreservehistory.org/essays/gold-convertibility-ends
- Friedman, M. (1992). Money mischief: Episodes in monetary history. Harcourt Brace.
- Friedman, M. (2006). The role of monetary policy. *The American Economic Review, 58*(1), 1–17.
- Galanter, M. (1984). Competing inequalities: Law and the backward classes in India. Oxford University Press.
- Hawtrey, R. G. (1933). The art of central banking. Longmans, Green and Co.
- Hodges, R. (2012). Money and power in the Middle Ages. Bloomsbury Academic.
- Jaffrelot, C. (2003). India's silent revolution: The rise of the lower castes in North India. Hurst & Company.
- Kedar, B. Z. (1996). The Templars and their sources of income. In B. Z. Kedar (Ed.), *The Horns of Hattin* (pp. 295–306). Boydell Press.
- Mayer, L. (1935). J.P. Morgan and the development of American finance. Harper & Row.
- Nicholson, H. J. (2001). The Knights Templar: A new history. Sutton Publishing.
- Niccol, A. (Director). (2011). *In time* [Film]. Regency Enterprises; New Regency Productions; Strike Entertainment.
- Nixon, R. (1971, August 15). *Address to the nation outlining a new economic policy: "The challenge of peace."* Papers of Richard M. Nixon. https://fraser.stlouisfed.org/archival-collection/papers-richard-m-nixon-1173/address-nation-outlining-a-new-economic-policy-3390

- Romanek, M. (Director). (2010). *Never let me go* [Film]. Fox Searchlight Pictures; DNA Films; Film4.
- Spielberg, S. (Director). (2018). *Ready Player One* [Film]. Warner Bros. Pictures; Amblin Entertainment; Amblin Partners; Village Roadshow Pictures; De Line Pictures; Farah Films & Management.
- Sveriges Riksbank. (2020). *First banknotes in Europe.* https://www.riksbank.se/en-gb/about-the-riksbank/history/historical-timeline/1600-1699/first-banknotes-in-europe/
- Thorat, S., & Newman, K. S. (2010). Blocked by caste: Economic discrimination in modern India. Oxford University Press.
- Villeneuve, D. (Director). (2017). *Blade Runner 2049* [Film]. Alcon Entertainment; Columbia Pictures; Scott Free Productions; Torridon Films; 16:14 Entertainment; Thunderbird Entertainment.
- Von Glahn, R. (2016). The economic history of China: From antiquity to the nineteenth century. Cambridge University Press.
- Wachowski, L., & Wachowski, L. (Directors). (1999). *The Matrix* [Film]. Warner Bros.; Village Roadshow Pictures; Groucho II Film Partnership; Silver Pictures.

www.ingramcontent.com/pod-product-compliance
Lightning Source LLC
LaVergne TN
LVHW022103200926
848481LV00003B/1051